THE MODERN WORLD
GENERAL EDITOR: C. H. C. BLOUNT

CHINA

BY

PING-CHIA KUO

OXFORD UNIVERSITY PRESS
1963

Oxford University Press, Amen House, London E.C.4

GLASGOW   NEW YORK   TORONTO   MELBOURNE   WELLINGTON
BOMBAY   CALCUTTA   MADRAS   KARACHI   LAHORE   DACCA
CAPE TOWN   SALISBURY   NAIROBI   IBADAN   ACCRA
KUALA LUMPUR   HONG KONG

PRINTED   IN   GREAT   BRITAIN   BY
NORTHUMBERLAND   PRESS   LIMITED
GATESHEAD   ON   TYNE

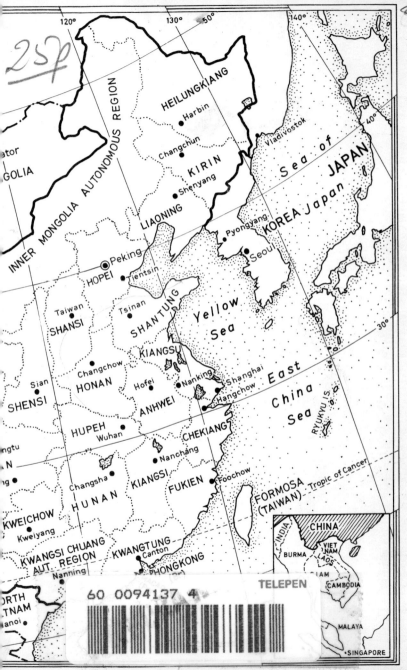

CONTENTS

LIST OF PLATES

Plates 1a, 1c and Plate 2 by courtesy of the *Radio Times* Hulton Picture Library; all the other Plates by courtesy of The Camera Press Ltd.

A NOTE ON PRONUNCIATION

In the transliteration of Chinese names, certain consonants are pronounced differently when aspirated (with an apostrophe) or unaspirated. Thus *ch*, *k*, *p*, *t*, and *ts* are pronounced like *j*, *g*, *b*, *d*, and *dz* respectively. When aspirated, *ch'*, *k'*, *p'*, *t'*, and *ts'* are pronounced like *ch*, *k*, *p*, *t*, and *ts* respectively, as in usual English pronunciation.

I

THE COUNTRY AND THE PEOPLE

FROM TIME TO TIME in the course of history China has fired the imagination of the world. Today, stirred into new life by the Communist revolution, she is again on the march. This great resurgence, however, represents a process of modernization more than anything else. The Communists are re-tooling an ancient civilization to turn it into a new world power. In spite of the revolution, they are compelled to work with the realities of China's physical setting and under the influence of the nation's experience and character. For this reason we must first examine the fundamental forces that dominate the life and work of the Chinese people.

Unlike other ancient civilizations that have vanished, China has a continuous history dating back four thousand years. The Chinese are among the world's most tenacious and resilient peoples. How do we account for this phenomenon? To a great extent this is due to her favourable environment. China is physically big. Her 3.8 million square miles of territory are forty times the size of the United Kingdom. It is larger than the United States, including Alaska and Hawaii. This immense domain has made it extremely difficult for China to be annihilated by other nations. On many historical occasions the Chinese saved their country from northern invaders by falling back on the southern provinces. During the Second World War they worsted Japan's occupation of the seaboard regions by basing their resistance on the far west. Defence in depth by 'trading space for time' is a formula which China has used time after time to ensure her survival.

China is also favourably situated. For the most part her territory is located in the temperate zone. The 2,500 mile north-south stretch falls within 18-54 degrees north latitude, while the 3,000-mile span between east and west lies within 73-135 degrees east longitude. This means that the Chinese people occupy what is perhaps the choicest part of Asia. Neither Arctic weather nor debilitating tropical heat inhibit their activities. Climatic conditions greatly aid the work and production of the people. As a result the Chinese have always enjoyed a margin of advantage in contests with other peoples along their borders. This is why the Chinese called their country the 'Middle Kingdom'. To them, their well-favoured land lay at the centre of the universe.

In addition to her magnificent environment China owes her strength to another asset, her vast manpower. The Chinese or Han people, marked by such distinctive features as black hair, prominent cheek bones, flat nose, and a pale yellow or olive complexion, form the largest branch of the Mongoloid or Yellow race. Throughout history China has outnumbered her neighbours. At the beginning of the Christian era she had a population of 50 million, while her enemy to the north, the Hsiung-nu, had 3 million. Today China has a population of 700 million, while Russia has 210 million and Japan 90 million. Some 13 million Chinese are also found overseas in South-East Asian countries. Population experts forecast that in fifty years every other person on earth may well be Chinese.

Such a large population indeed leads to great pressure on the land and to a low standard of living. Yet it is a sustaining force for the nation in a real sense. In the Second World War, for instance, prolonged resistance against Japan was made possible by huge reserves of manpower. Recent statistics show that men of military age in China have topped the 90 million mark, as compared with 40 million in Soviet Russia, 30 million in the United States, and 8 million in the United Kingdom. There is an unspoken faith in the minds of the people that in an hour of great peril their sheer numbers will enable them to find a way out.

In times of peace, too, China's huge manpower has been a source of strength in the struggle against nature and in all manner of public works and engineering. From the building of the Great Wall and the digging of the Grand Canal to the cutting of the Burma Road over dangerous mountains and harnessing the waters of the Yellow River, the utilization of the nation's manpower has been a potent factor in national power. More significant still, as China acquires new manufacturing plants her massive labour force will out-produce other nations by lowering the cost of production. This is a sobering prospect which no one can afford to ignore.

China, then, is twice blessed—first, in her physical size, and second, in the number of her people. Yet not every part of this vast territory is equally useful nor is the population evenly spread over the country. Both in topography and in the distribution of her population China is lopsided. Plains are found only in the eastern third of the country. The vast expanse of her west is taken up by the high mountains of Tibet and Sinkiang, and by the desert and steppe of the Mongolian upland. Since these mountains, plateaux, and deserts are not suitable for agriculture, over ninety per cent. of the total population live in the twenty provinces in the eastern third of the country (generally known as China Proper), while less than ten per cent. are thinly spread over Tibet, Sinkiang, and Inner Mongolia, the three large outlying regions. Hence there are, in effect, two Chinas : agricultural China in the east, with very dense population; and non-agricultural China in the west, with very sparse population.

In non-agricultural China the people's occupation is pastoral. These regions have been left by the Chinese to certain non-Chinese or non-Han minority groups, who are accustomed to a nomadic life. Thus some two million followers of Lamaism inhabit Tibet, whose 500,000 square miles of territory are a huge mass of mountains, high, dry, cold, and barren. Sinkiang, in the west, contains 650,000 square miles, and is cut in two by the T'ien Shan range. The northern part, known as Dzungaria, is inhabited by a half million Kazaks, a pastoral people akin to their brethren in Soviet Central Asia; while the southern part, known as the Tarim Basin, is inhabited by four million Uighurs, who are a Turkic people believing in Mohammedanism. Finally, Inner Mongolia, in the north, extends over 300,000 square miles. Except for its southern fringe, with a precarious wheat economy, it is typical steppe country, where one and a half million Mongols, also believers in Lamaism, roam with their herds of camels, sheep, and cattle.

Through the ages the Chinese government, based in China Proper, never developed a truly effective technique of holding these dependencies with their non-agricultural mode of living. Today the situation is changing under the Communist régime. Not only are industries, railways, and highways being built in all these regions, but the age-old attitude of neglect is being replaced by a policy of active integration. By and large, however, these regions still remain non-agricultural, and are still thinly populated by non-Han peoples.

As we turn to agricultural China, we find a totally different world. This is the real China (hence the term China Proper). As we have noted above, more than ninety per cent. of the population live in this part of the country. Although here and there we find pockets of non-Han groups, the population is composed overwhelmingly of the Chinese or Han people. Here is the stage on which the drama of forty centuries of Chinese history has been played. The central fact which dominates one's sight and mind is that the livelihood of the toiling masses is dependent on agriculture. The success or failure of the crops literally means life or death for countless millions of people. The people are closely identified with Mother Earth. Agriculture colours every aspect of their life, and shapes their aspirations and sense of values.

Chinese agriculture is characterized by a great sense of urgency, on account of the limited extent of cultivable land. We have said that China Proper is agricultural. But even here seventy per cent. of the map area is unsuitable for farming. The Tsingling range separating North and Central China, the Nanling range separating Central and South China, and other mountain systems that jut eastward toward the sea cover an enormous part of the terrain, causing high elevations, low temperatures, or inadequate rainfall. As a result the agricultural regions are found only in the lowlands in close proximity to the major rivers, notably the Yellow River in North China, the Yangtze in Central China, and the Pearl River in South China.

Wherever such a region exists, therefore, it is of vital importance to the people. Unfortunately there are barely a dozen such regions. In the north, with cooler climate and less rainfall, there are three major regions: the Yellow River plain; the Wei and Fen valleys in the loess highlands (deposits of fine sands carried in by winds from Central Asia); and the Liao River valley in South Manchuria. These are producers of wheat and kaoliang (a variety of sorghum), plus sizeable crops of soya bean and millet. In Central China rice is the staple crop, on account of the warmer climate and more abundant rainfall. Here we find four major regions. The lower Yangtze plain, which produces rice in summer plus a crop of wheat in winter, has the heaviest population density in the country. The Szechwan basin, along the upper Yangtze, is a rich rice country; it was known as 'Heavenly Treasure' 天府之 throughout history, while during the Second World War Chiang Kai-shek relied on this area as the base for Chinese resistance. The Central Lakes region, in the middle Yangtze valley, rivals Szechwan in its heavy rice production and is celebrated as China's 'Rice Bowl'. The last region in this group is the Chekiang-Fukien area along the south-eastern seaboard, which is a rice-and-tea double cropping region.

As one moves farther south past the Nanling range into Kwangtung, the countryside is humid and sub-tropical. The Pearl River valley and the Canton delta have over sixty inches of rain per year and a growing season so long that the farmers raise three crops of rice, or eight crops of vegetables. The provinces further inland from Kwangtung constitute the South-West rice area. Though hilly and less fertile, the rice production of this region supports the vast hinterland in the south-west.

True, each of these regions yields a picture of great fertility and productivity. But the total acreage under cultivation is all too limited. It was estimated to be 220 million acres in the nineteen-thirties; 280 million acres at the close of the nineteen-fifties. These are surprisingly low figures, considering the size of China's population. The United States supports her 180 million people with the products of 360 million acres. In China, on the other hand, 700 million people have to live off these 280 million acres. Cultivated land per person in the United States is two acres, whereas in China it is four-tenths of an acre. In terms of cultivated land the average population density of China is over 1,500 per square mile. In the delta areas there are as many as 2,500 persons per square mile. It is this tremendous pressure of population on the land that gives to Chinese agriculture a sense of urgency.

Chinese agriculture further suffers from pre-modern methods of farming. Unlike his European or American counter-part, the Chinese peasant depends on the power of his muscles and of draught animals (the water buffalo in Central and South China; the donkey and mule in North China) in the cultivation of the land. His tools are primitive and crude: they scarcely extend beyond the hoe, the spade, and the plough. Since labour is cheap and in over-supply, he finds that he can better afford to wear out human muscles than to buy even the simplest farm machinery. An agricultural worker in Europe has at his command twenty to twenty-five horse-power, and puts in two days of labour per acre of wheat. The Chinese peasant, on the other hand, has only one horse-power at his command, and must put in thirty days of labour per acre of wheat. The result is intensive farming in the truest sense of the term, the concentrated application of human labour on very limited areas of choice land. The slowness of this type of work virtually rules out the utilization of poorer lands. It calls for many workers to cultivate a small farm in order to complete the work routine within the growing season, and lays stress on the ever-growing need to increase the per-unit yield by all conceivable means, such as irrigation, double-cropping, etc.

One really needs to visit the scene to realize how hard the Chinese peasants work in order to make a living. Perhaps the most poignant picture of intensive farming is to be found in the rice fields of Central and South China. Rice is the favourite crop of the Chinese because it returns the heaviest yield per acre, and in these crowded regions it offers the best hope of winning the necessary quantity of food from the land. The cycle of rice culture begins in late June, when seeds are planted in nursery plots. During the thirty-odd days required for the seeds to grow, the peasant population of the whole village is mobilized to prepare the paddy fields by breaking and smoothing the soil and irrigating the field. This is all done by hand with the assistance of the hoe. It takes four or five days for one man to prepare one-third of an acre of paddy field. Surrounded by dikes, the field is constantly flooded. Water buffaloes, blindfolded, may be seen turning huge water wheels. Wooden buckets hang from these wheels and lift the water, via an enclosed escalator, from a nearby canal or stream into the fields. Often human feet supply the necessary power. When the rice shoots are ready, they are transplanted. On this hopeful and joyous occasion the villagers plant together in what is essentially group farming, working and singing in unison. After the transplanting, weeding and pumping water form the daily chore. The peasants work barefoot in mud and water. In September the rice blooms, and by the end of the month it ripens. During the following month the field is drained of water. Then come the final stages of cutting, threshing, hulling, and polishing.

Such hard work on the part of the peasant masses, however, has not provided a way out of the question of population pressure on the land. Nor has the socialization of agriculture by the Communists, which we shall discuss in a later chapter, substantially altered the situation. The crowded areas grow more crowded. The countless millions of farm hands work harder today than before, in an attempt to increase the per-unit production of food grains. Even with the introduction of better cropping programmes and of improved tools, the 'Great Leap Forward' campaign was in essence a further intensification of intensive farming. Whatever increase took place in food grain production was achieved through the more diligent application of human muscles and through the more intensive use of the soil.

Perhaps to a larger extent than other systems of farming, Chinese agriculture is exposed to tremendous risks. Since a satisfactory harvest hangs upon the non-interruption of the delicate time-table of human labour, any upset in climatic conditions may bring disaster. The Chinese farmer is almost entirely at the mercy of nature. Too little rainfall holds the threat of drought. Excessive rainfall causes rivers to overflow their banks, turning the fields into lakes. Both destroy crops and bring famine to millions. The incidence of floods along the Yellow River is especially high because of the heavy accumulation of silt in the river bed. It was good fortune that the first nine years of Communist rule were relatively free from such natural calamities. But the severe droughts and floods from mid-1959 to mid-1961 caused famine in many areas, and consequently set back economic planning in all sectors. The Peking government has launched numerous projects for flood control and for irrigation. They will no doubt help the situation. But so long as China's enormous population is crowded within the limited arable areas, distress caused by nature's havocs will continue to be one of her basic problems.

Now we must leave agriculture and turn to the urban life of the Chinese people. There are literally thousands of cities and towns. First of all there is Peking, the capital. This perennially majestic city, renowned for its palaces, temples, and towers, has a charm combining mellowness with spirit. It may be regarded as the epitome of the most exalted elements in Chinese civilization. Then there are ancient capitals with vanished splendour, such as Sian, Loyang, and Kaifeng, some regaining strength in this new age, others continuing untouched by the changes of the times. In every province one or more centres of metropolitan size will be found, each a capital city of its region. Among these we may note Nanking, Changsha, Chengtu, Kweilin, Chungking, Taiyuan, Mukden, and Urumchi. Modern commercial centres are for the most part located along the coast or along the lower course of the rivers. Shanghai, Tientsin, Canton, and Hankow are among the outstanding cities in this group. Shanghai, in particular, is an enormous city with a population of seven million. Finally, we must remember the booming industrial cities. Among these, Paotow, Chengchow, and Lanchow deserve special mention.

Life in the Chinese cities is busy, active, and colourful. Shops and vendors with their infinite variety of items for trade line the streets. Restaurants with delectable cuisine and theatres displaying native dramas and motion pictures cater for the public. Noise and crowds appear to be the inevitable accompaniments of city life in China. In years past cleanliness and public sanitation were grievously neglected. Under the communist régime intensive drives for public health have revolutionized the situation. Today Chinese cities are among the cleanest in the world. But boulevards with modern pavements are few. Most city streets are still the old, narrow flagged lanes. Men travel about either on foot or in pedicabs. There is building activity in the newer cities—building to house new industrial plants and their workers. But, by and large, the typical skyline of a Chinese city is devoid of tall structures of the modern type.

Until recent years the urban centres in China resembled the medieval towns of Europe rather than its modern cities. They were emporiums for the exchange of farmers' produce and village handicrafts brought in from the countryside, rather than of manufactured goods made in the cities themselves. They were also administrative centres, as the scholar-gentry class who served as government officials made their homes in them. Since these were men with leisure for study and enjoyment, many devoted their talents to calligraphy, painting, and the composition of essays and poems, while others became patrons of the theatre, the arts, and literature. Today, the old scholar-gentry class has been replaced by Communist party workers. But the cities remain the strongholds of the bureacratic and managerial personnel. The growth of in-dustries and the influx of factory workers are indeed changing the traditional appearance of Chinese cities. Still there is nothing resembling the gigantic industrial complexes characteristic of urban centres in the West. The Communist policy encourages milliards of small rural in-dustries and fosters considerable independence of the country from the city.

One of the great weaknesses of China is poor transporta-tion. Today China has only 20,000 miles of railways and 300,000 miles of motor highways. For everyday travel and transport the masses depend on the age-old dirt roads, and rivers, lakes, and canals. But since the old roads are not more than five feet wide, overland traffic is carried mainly by wheel-barrow. As for water transport, the sailing craft are mostly junks or sampans, which are extremely low in both speed and capacity. The overall picture of trans-portation in China, then, is pre-modern. Railways, motor vehicles, steamers, or airplanes are beyond the reach of most people. The prevalent scene across the country is movement on draught animals, junks, wheel-barrows or human carriers. This type of transportation is not only too costly, but too time-consuming. Twenty miles represent the maximum distance that can be travelled in a day by any one of these means. The vast majority of peasants do their selling and buying in market towns within a day's walk. Few of them ever move beyond a radius of 100 miles throughout their lives.

Just as the crowding of population and intensive farming lend a sense of urgency to Chinese agriculture, so does this poor state of transportation make for regional differences and cultural lags. Low mobility renders Chinese society sedentary; each region tends to be a world in itself. This explains the amazing variety of dialects, folkways, and provincial traits. For instance, the northerner, accustomed to wheat or kaoliang, the mule-drawn cart, the desert wind from the Gobi, and the elegant Mandarin speech, is ill at ease in Central or South China, where everything seems strange to him: the all-rice diet, travel by river boats, the Wu and Cantonese dialects, and even the humid, subtropical air. Such inter-regional barriers have begun to break down in recent years, but China still is a country of striking contrasts.

The improvement of transportation is of necessity a halting process. Not only does the construction of modern means of transport take time, but the inertia of the old days has a tendency to slow down the momentum of change. This is why many cultural lags persist in this age of transition. Travellers in great cities like Shanghai and Canton will find large department stores, modern municipal facilities, and even a few giant industrial plants. Yet a short distance beyond the city boundaries one finds age-old villages, with dingy shops, handicraft factories in hovels, and homes burning vegetable oil lamps. Although opportunities have been opened to Chinese women, winning for them equal rights with men, their psychology and sense of values are still those of the old days, because they have not yet thrown off the memory of their inferior position. In matters of education, there are the most advanced higher institutions of learning; yet the masses are struggling to emerge from illiteracy, with thousands of spare-time schools teaching them the rudiments of reading and writing. In medicine, Western-style doctors and clinics operate alongside herb doctors, using herb medicines with which Chinese ailments have been treated for centuries. These bizarre facets of a nation in transition drive home one strong conclusion. Although change is to be seen on every hand, the weight of old ways still lies heavily over all.

In these circumstances the living standard of the masses is necessarily low. Almost everyone in China is poor. Income per head has, in effect, never exceeded £16 a year. Yet the Chinese have never lost spirit on account of poverty. This is an important point in understanding China. Those who use the Western yardstick to measure the threat of want in China must remember that there is a great difference in the psychology of the two societies. The Chinese have lived with their standard of living for many centuries. They are prepared to live with it for many more. In their long travail they have developed these responses: frugality, patience, industriousness, a sense of humour, and above all, a philosophical approach to the realities of life. These are the qualities that make the Chinese tough and persevering, that give them the will to live and fight against poverty.

Better than any other people, the Chinese know how to wage a defensive rather than an offensive battle in life. Unable to expand his income and ever aware of the hardships of earning a livelihood, the average Chinese makes the most of life within the framework of austerity. He creates happiness by making fewer demands for himself. Poverty thus becomes a relative thing for him. If the landless and hungry peasant of yesterday is assured a secure ration, he becomes immediately charged with hope and enthusiasm, even if he enjoys no luxury in material things or in individual political rights. Further, since poverty has persisted so long, it has lost much of its sting. On the gates of many a village hut one reads the motto: 'Contentment with what we have is the key to happiness.' The Chinese society is not an acquisitive society. Opportunities are scarce and success never spectacular. People yearn more for peace and stability to provide a climate for work than for affluence or wealth for the sake of pleasure. This is one of the major differences in temperament which has made mutual understanding difficult between China and the West.

Like other civilizations, the Chinese civilization is shaped by the physical and social environment of the people and their responses to that environment. These factors, being quite different from their counterparts in Europe and America, have produced a civilization in China quite different in kind from that of the West. The accent of life in the West is on the individual, on his fight to subdue nature, on his search for his own salvation, on the quest for progress based on competition with other individuals. In the life and environment of China none of these has been stressed. From what we have observed—the dependence on agriculture, the density of population, and the intensive mode of making a living—the factors conditioning life lead to the central point that group endeavour and proper group behaviour occupy a place of overriding importance in the Chinese scene. Under these circumstances the Chinese have worked out a way of life which stresses co-operation and balance in the relation of man to man, upholds order and harmony with nature, accepts the subordination of the individual to the group, and follows a secular rather than a metaphysical outlook upon life. It is here that we must look for the key to an understanding of Chinese society and life.

As one travels through villages and towns, farms and factories, schools and hospitals, one cannot help but notice such psychological processes at work. There is a tacit recognition among the people that their destiny is tied to a social structure which makes accommodation to the workings of nature and of man imperative. People fear the consequences of uncontrolled social tensions and therefore follow a course of co-operation. The Chinese have probably the best grasp of the true meaning of the word, reciprocity. The Westerner believes in doing to others what others would do to him. The Chinese, on the other hand, refrains from doing to others what he does not wish others to do to him. In a very real sense this is the teaching of Confucius at work, even though today everything is under Communist direction. For Confucius taught the people to observe their respective positions and status for the sake of achieving the best social order. And the masses are doing precisely that under the Communist government.

We shall discuss the life and teachings of Confucius in the next chapter. But it is well to note here that Confucianism best exemplifies the spirit of Chinese civilization. Today we hear much about Confucius being repudiated by the Communists. Actually, what has been overthrown is the Confucianist state, or its political and economic practices. The ethical teachings of the great sage are as valid a part of Chinese life now as they were in the past. Confucianism is to the Chinese people what the Bible is to the Western world. As it is actually practised in the daily life of the Chinese people, the concepts of co-operation and reciprocity, mentioned above, are stressed. In addition, emphasis is placed on certain virtues: kindliness, righteousness, propriety, intelligence, and loyalty. The objective is to strive for a harmonious social order by regulating the relations of man to man and to nature. If we put all these virtues together, they add up to moderation, which is another way of saying the curtailment of individual ambition.

Such a social attitude, unlike the social attitude in the West, prompts the people to behave well within the group.

This is as true of the small child and the teen-ager as of the adult. Although Chinese children work and play as do children the world over, they have a sense of their place in the group. This has hardly had to be enforced by discipline. As a result Chinese children are quieter and more docile than their counterparts in other lands. The teenager, too, is courteous and responsible. Whether he is at work, at study, or at play, he responds in the measure expected by the group. There is little juvenile delinquency. Adults, likewise, show a strong sense of proper behaviour. Among them such crimes as assault, murder, and drunkenness are seldom known. One would expect the incidence of crime and delinquency to be higher on account of the crowded and hard conditions of living. Yet it appears to be lower because of them. To be humble and polite toward one's fellow man, to exert an unfailing effort to make an art of living, is the spirit of the social code governing the Chinese people, whether in the traditional society or under the present régime.

One wonders how such a state of affairs could have been achieved, considering the widespread illiteracy and the lack of effective political organization in the traditional society. The answer is two-fold. First, the Chinese believe in education by example or in learning through living. The formula is for the *élite*—the ' princely man '—to lead, and for the masses to follow his direction, even as ' grass bends before the wind '. Such a process by-passes formal instruction, yet guides the entire people to right conduct in their everyday life. It is the direct method of teaching applied on a massive scale. Thus a unique and powerful social code permeates the Chinese character. This is why the Chinese people are cultivated without being literate, and the Chinese society never primitive or crude, but highly sophisticated.

The second factor is the vital role played by the family

in implementing the social code. Until the Communists came to power the family was the all-important social unit in China. It was much larger and performed many more functions than the conjugal family of today, consisting of husband, wife, and their children. Embracing not only father and mother, but grandparents, children, grand-children, uncles, aunts, and cousins, the traditional family was an integral unit of production and consumption. Earnings formed a common fund; every member received support from it; and responsibility was shared by all. Naturally, this became the training ground for group behaviour. The social code mentioned above was rigorously enforced. The oldest member of the family was the patriarch, the centre of authority and respect. Age was held in esteem; filial piety and ancestor worship were considered fundamental virtues. A child's marriage, his career, and his entire course of action were determined by the family group. From this we can see why in the teachings of Confucius a sound family system was regarded as the base for good government.

Today the Communists have revolutionized the system of production and consumption. The large traditional family has shrunk. The home no longer houses several generations, but contains only the conjugal family. Many functions of the traditional family have been taken over by the party and the state. For instance, the state sanctions marriages through civil registration. The commune-operated kindergarten cares for the children. The party worker fosters the moral code and discipline. For employment, jobs are assigned by the state or the party. Filial piety and ancestor worship are dead. Rather than revering age, the nation has turned to the young and looks to them for the work needed to create the new socialist order.

The changes are indeed drastic. Nevertheless, the underlying logic remains the same. The same insistence on proper group behaviour is being implemented by agencies other than the old family. In place of the old family loyalty, there is now substituted a new loyalty to the state. Underlying the change is the same acceptance of orders from above, the same subordination of the individual to the group. So long as the social framework remains what it is, group support of directives from the top will mean surer guarantees of the common good than will the assertion of individual independence. This explains why a paternalistic government, whether of the old or the new type, finds a favourable climate in Chinese society. In this sense the disappearance of the old family will not alter the spirit of Chinese civilization in any considerable degree.

In their spiritual life the Chinese people are marked by a strong secularism. This does not mean that the Chinese are incapable of religious experience. From classical antiquity they have inherited a belief in Heaven and in the spirits of nature, as well as the cult of ancestral souls. But, characteristically, they have given all of these a utilitarian turn to serve life in this world. To them, Heaven and the spirits administer rewards and punishments, while ancestral souls are of necessity the lord-protectors of the living. Taoism did not last long as a naturalistic philosophy, but was transformed into a body of magic, alchemy, and occultism promising longevity or other practical benefits to the people. Buddhism spread far and wide among the people. But the Chinese zest for life could not tolerate its insistence on asceticism, celibacy, and annihilation of desire. So its tenets were twisted beyond recognition. As Buddhism is observed among the Chinese masses, it is a handy cult using repetitive prayers before idols to bring succour during sickness or distress. Christianity, too, after three centuries of missionary work, could not claim more than five million converts at any one time, out of a total population of several hundred million. The most illuminating commentary is the fact that many Chinese see nothing strange in being Confucianist, Buddhist, and Taoist at one and the same time.

The only body of teachings which the Chinese have accepted without reservation is Confucianism, which as we have seen, is rationalistic and humanistic. Such secularism in the Chinese temperament means that something other than religion has fulfilled the spiritual needs of the people. The Chinese regard the striving for moral perfection as the highest purpose of life. It may take the form of kindliness towards one's fellow man, or it may take the form of filial piety towards one's parents. In either case it assumes the form of a creed based on powerful moral sanctions, but without the benefit of gods. This is the strength of Chinese secularism. Having worked out this rationalistic system, the Chinese give little thought to the salvation of the individual soul. They do not entertain a concept of God as the creator of the universe or of man. They are not concerned with a sense of sin. For the most part they shun metaphysical teachings. Confucius' whole philosophy is this-worldly. He said: 'Not knowing enough about life, how can we talk about death?'

The Chinese owe much to this secularism in their intellectual tradition. Religion in the form of an organized Church has not succeeded in maintaining itself among them. Religious wars are unknown in Chinese history. Here a comparison with India is illuminating. The fusion of races in India ended in ethnic compartments, linguistic groups, and especially in the caste system, because Hinduism gave sanction to the separation of social groups based on hereditary occupations. This caused civil strife, bloodshed, and failure to achieve unity or stability. Thanks to her secularism, the history of China is marked by tolerance and an open-mindedness of spirit. It is a history of assimilation, not segregation. China has operated on the premise of the equality and homogeneity of all peoples, and has not shut her doors against any group that could find itself at peace with her ways. So despite many woes in other directions, China has evolved and maintained a unified nation based on a homogeneous culture for at least two thousand years.

What, then, gives China the individuality that sets her apart from other nations and inspires her people with an unfailing vitality and dynamism? The answer has been suggested in the preceding paragraph: she is not only a nation, but an independent culture representing a separate and complete entity in itself. China has grown during long centuries of isolation from other centres of population. This has given her civilization an indigenous and insular character. The best illustration of this point is the Chinese language. In its in-grown and isolating qualities there is nothing in the world like it. It is a language based on ideographs, has no alphabet, and is monosyllabic. Since the entire language does not contain many sounds, one sound has to perform the functions of many words, for which reason different tones are established to round out an adequate vocabulary. To further complicate the matter, grammatical relations are shown not by conjugations or inflections, but by word order and context. Each ideograph represents an object or an idea, and one requires the knowledge of some 3,000 such individual characters to read an ordinary book. All in all, it is an extremely difficult language to master unless one has grown up with it. Moreover, the vocabulary formed by these ideographs is peculiarly adapted to Chinese thought and imagery. So to outsiders this language has always been a strong barrier against attempts to communicate with the Chinese; for the Chinese themselves it has proved a tremendous force for cultural cohesion and continuity. As we have said earlier, there are many local dialects of colloquial Chinese. But in written Chinese one and only one language is used throughout the country.

The in-grown qualities of Chinese culture, however, tell only half of the story. On the other side of the ledger, the development of Chinese culture in isolation has made it a complete whole. Not only has it a personality of its own, but it embraces a comprehensive treasure of human experience and wisdom which at least in that part of the world have answered man's needs well. For this reason China has always claimed, subconsciously perhaps, the right to be the radiating centre of a cultural empire. On numerous occasions alien peoples and ideas that made their way into China succumbed to the superior influence of her culture. In fact China came to rely on this ability to assimilate her invaders rather than on her military strength to subdue them. Looking abroad, her leaders and thinkers confidently assumed that what was good for China would be good for all the peoples of East Asia. In the halcyon days of the empire her cultural patterns were exported to Korea, Japan, and Vietnam, where they were invariably a leavening force for imitation or reform. So China is extrovert as well as introvert. Whether it is called leadership or chauvinism, the lengthening shadow of China's example seems destined to spread across her neighbouring lands whenever she enters an era of impressive achievement.

It is important to keep in mind these powerful and enduring forces in Chinese civilization. What the Communists are doing today is to re-examine their applicability to twentieth century conditions, keeping whatever is useful and supplying whatever is wanting. In the following chapters we shall see that they are modernizing the country by developing organization and technology, the two areas where China's traditional civilization is weaker than Western civilization. Aside from these, they are far from sweeping away China's ancient heritage. On the contrary, the timeless factors in the nation's environment and psychology are being further exploited to make the new China a stronger China on the world scene. The power of Chinese civilization, leading in the directions of both internal cohesion and external expansion, is as clearly in evidence today as it was in the past.

2

THE LEGACY OF THE PAST

THE ORIGINS OF the Chinese people go back to remote antiquity. As long as half a million years ago an early Paleolithic culture flourished near Peking. However, historians are not certain that it was the direct forerunner of Chinese civilization. For the authenticated beginnings of society and culture, we must begin with the Chinese of the Neolithic Age who lived in the Yellow River plain from 4,000-2,000 B.C. During this age, the people, organized in tribes and living in river valleys, developed agriculture as the basis of their existence, with millet, wheat, and dry rice as the staple crops. They also kept domesticated animals, made pottery, and acquired the art of making silk. This was the start of the civilized life of the Chinese people.

From about 2,000 B.C. the Chinese began to use bronze, and for the next fourteen centuries they became superb casters of bronze weapons and sacrificial vessels. During this long span of time, which we call the Bronze Age, the early society made continuous progress, taking on new and complex institutions. The first phase of progress was made under the Shang, a kingdom that out-grew tribal rule and controlled the territory in present day Honan and Shantung. Agriculture made notable strides. Settled village life, intensive farming, and group co-operation for flood control took permanent form. The Shang ruler led in battle and in the hunt, acted as a priest between man and nature in special sacrifices, and created a bureaucracy to take charge of irrigation works, grain storage, and other public responsibilities. Cities, too, began to develop as centres for administration and for the exchange of agricultural products.

Being worshippers of ancestral souls, the Shang people practised divination. Questions were written on animal bones or tortoise shells, which were heated to make cracks; the cracks were then interpreted for ancestral guidance. The pictographic-ideographic characters inscribed on these 'oracle bones' were the earliest written form of the Chinese language. The questions written on the bones gave us the names of the Shang rulers and glimpses of Shang life. Indeed the diviners were the first generation of China's educators. They were the custodians of knowledge: from their works arose astronomy, mathematics, chronology, history, political economy, philosophy, and literature.

In 1027 B.C. the Shang was overthrown by the Chou, a new power from Shensi in the west. The Chou ruled the vast realm with a feudal system which gave a new direction and a new stimulus to the development of Chinese society. Politically, the Chou turned over the conquered territory of the plain as feudal grants to the members and relatives of the Chou clan and allied chieftains, tying them to the Chou by the bonds of investiture and vassalage and using primogeniture to provide for the orderly transfer of power within the states. Economically, there was a high degree of well-being among the peasants, because land was owned by the state and was periodically redistributed to take care of population changes. Thus the Chou society was a peaceable society owing to the relative absence of tension among the masses.

The Chou brought with them the worship of a Heaven which rewarded the pious and punished the wicked. This belief in retribution, along with the prevailing worship of the spirits of nature connected with fertility and production, was compounded with Shang ancestor worship to form a vast pantheon.[1] But these religious practices, developed under the influence of the agricultural community and family life, did not deal with creation or salvation. Their purpose was to foster and fortify routine existence in this world.

The more positive force of Chou culture was education. With economic tension kept at a minimum, the Chou leaders taught the people to follow an ethical code in their daily life. Indeed schools were developed. But those not privileged to learn reading and writing were educated under the example of recognized social usages. Rituals for every occasion were worked out to promote etiquette and decorum. Music was used as a medium to inspire virtuous thoughts and behaviour. The entire philosophy was to better group conduct through the cultivation of character. Thus there was cultural flow and advance as well as social well-being. This is why men like Confucius later looked back to this era with nostalgia as a model social order.

Chou feudalism, however, had no power for unification. As the feudal lords fought among themselves and as the Chou ruler lost his domain to barbarian invaders (771 B.C.), the old order fell apart, giving way to changes on many fronts. Political power was seized by one feudal state after another. As warfare intensified, armies grew larger, while cavalry replaced chariots. With the introduction of iron in the sixth century B.C., sharper swords were made, further contributing to the scourge of war. In the period of the Warring States (453-221 B.C.) China suffered heavily from chaos and bloodshed.

More important still were the changes on the economic and social fronts. The introduction of copper coins stimulated trade, and gave rise to a money economy dominated by an independent merchant class. As a result, land became an asset to be bought and sold. The beneficiaries

[1] An assembly of gods.

were businessmen and scholars, who acted in haste to obtain land as their private property. The aristocrats lost their former fiefs and sub-fiefs. As for the peasant masses, since their tenancy on the land was no longer assured, many became unemployed and begged for hire. So the old society of hereditary aristocrats and commoners was now supplanted by a new society consisting of the landlord-scholars in government and the unprivileged peasant masses.

Now we are entering the most creative period in the history of Chinese civilization. The impact of these changes on men's minds gave rise to an era of great philosophers, to whom China is indebted for her rich intellectual heritage. Of the numerous teachers and thinkers, Lao-tzu, originator of the Taoist philosophy, represented a negative reaction to the prevailing disorder. He scorned the conventions and beliefs of the Chou, and in their place advocated harmony with nature, which he called 'tao' or 'the way'. This harmony was to be sought not by exertion, but by non-action. He held that human nature would find its own equilibrium if left to itself, and that the remedy for the times was not strong government, but less government of any kind.

In contrast to Lao-tzu's protests, the teachings of Confucius presented programmes for positive action. These were the teachings that exerted the deepest influence on Chinese civilization in subsequent ages. Born in Shantung in 551 B.C., Confucius received an excellent education in his childhood and youth, and ultimately became the greatest of all China's teachers. His teaching brought him many disciples, by whom his ideas were spread far and wide throughout the country. Tradition says that he compiled and edited the classics of ancient times: the *Canon of History*; the *Book of Odes*; the *Book of Changes*; the *Record of Rites*; and the *Spring and Autumn Annals*.

These works, together with the 'Four Books' containing the philosophical and moral teachings of Confucius himself and of Mencius (see below), constitute the standard treasury of Confucian thought that served to educate countless millions down to our own time.

Unwilling to revolt, historically minded, and humanist at heart, Confucius was an admirer of the old order of the Chou. He strove to perpetuate the ethical practices and principles which had proved workable under that order. The heart of his teaching stressed man's place in society rather than the individual himself. Confucius held that peace and order in a human community should be based on the maintenance of basic social relationships, which in turn depended upon the observance of status and position. Yet rather than use coercion for the achievement of this objective, he recommended education and persuasion as the better approach.

Clearly Confucius was the philosopher of the Centre, just as Lao-tzu was the philosopher of the Left. The philosopher of the Right was another eminent thinker, Mo-tzu, who had no use for either Taoist cynicism or Confucianist ritual and formalism. With a conviction approaching religion, he believed in a supreme Will of Heaven, which should be fulfilled by practising universal love. If love were extended to all alike, without regard to family or social barriers, Mo-tzu held that a firmer basis would be built for peace and order. To him war was wasteful and senseless. His ideal commonweal rested upon economy and simplicity. These teachings indeed contained profound truths, but they presented no concrete programme for implementation.

In each of these schools the teachings of the founder received amplification by disciples or supporters. Mencius and Hsün-tzu, for example, elaborated the Confucian teachings, as Ch'uang-tzu elaborated the Taoist teachings.

However, among the disciples of Hsün-tzu, Han-fei-tzu and Li Ssu founded yet another school of philosophy, the Legalist school. Seeing the need for complete control and unity, this school advocated an absolutist state, with severe laws and punishments. Thorough regimentation of the people, subordination of the subject to the state, outlawry of any separatist movements—these were among the panaceas put forth by this group. As far as the Legalists were concerned, no amount of Machiavellianism could be too much for the sake of strengthening the power of the prince and of the state.

It was of great importance that China produced these thinkers, who rose out of the chaos with systems of thought that could serve as beacons for the nation's future growth. The soul-searching was done when it was most needed. Henceforth China was never to feel poor in so far as her spiritual foundations were concerned. One of the Warring States, the Ch'in, actually followed the Legalist philosophy and opened a fresh page in Chinese history. It was probably the world's oldest totalitarian state. Its leaders stimulated population growth, built irrigation works, forced all subjects into productive occupations, and won control over the food-producing basin in Szechwan. Thanks to these measures the Ch'in subdued its rivals one after another, until in 221 B.C. Shih Huang-ti (the First Emperor) brought the entire country into a unified empire (hence the subsequent use of the name 'China'). This was the high point in the evolution of ancient China. A way

1. (a) *Confucius* (*551-479* B.C.). Portrait painting in China did not begin until about 400 years after the time of Confucius, so all likenesses of him are imaginary.
   (b) *Sun Yat-sen* (*1866-1925*). 'Father of the Chinese Revolution' and founder of the Kuomintang political party.
   (c) *Chiang Kai-shek* (*1887-   *). Leader of the Kuomintang after the death of Sun Yat-sen.
   (d) *Mao Tse-tung* (*1893-   *). Leader of the Chinese Communist Party.

32

1a

1b

1c

1d

2

—imperial unification—was now found to end the chaos that followed the dissolution of Chou feudalism.

For the sake of absolute control Shih Huang-ti resorted to certain excesses, such as the burning of classics and persecution of scholars who extolled the past. But these measures were more than offset by his most enduring contribution, the creation of a unified and centralized empire. He divided the country into commanderies (medium-sized provinces), which in turn were divided into districts, and governed them with a trinity of officials appointed by the central government—a civil administrator, a military governor, and a controller. Then he extended the frontiers of the empire. The Ch'in armies subdued the territories along the coast as far south as North Vietnam and established control over the Middle Yangtze valley. Roads were built to link the far-flung outposts with the capital. Throughout the empire he enforced uniform systems of law, language, weights and measures.

Even more stupendous were the defence measures in the north. As a massive barrier to keep out the Hsiung-nu or Huns of Mongolia, the Ch'in built the famous Great Wall by combining and adding to the walls erected in earlier ages. For this purpose hundreds of thousands of convict labourers were sent to the front, plus a quarter of a million soldiers to guard the wall. Built of stone, brick, and earth, it was 1,500 miles long (stretching from Kansu to the Manchurian coast), twenty feet high, with a roadway fifteen feet wide on top, dotted every few hundred yards with fortified towers. This gigantic feat demonstrated what massive manpower could accomplish.

The Ch'in was overthrown by popular revolts following the death of Shih Huang-ti, because his measures of iron

2. *The Temple of Heaven, Peking*. Built about 1420 to a design already thought ancient during the Han dynasty. Extensively restored during the eighteenth century.

and blood were too much for the people. However, the Han dynasty which took over in 206 B.C. immediately consolidated control, with Ch'ang-an (Sian) as its capital. Thus the framework of the unified empire was carried forward intact. By building on the base of the Ch'in's achievements the Han ruled for four hundred years, ushering in one of the most memorable epochs in Chinese history. With the Han the development of ancient China reached its climax. In power and glory the Han empire was easily a rival of its contemporary, the Roman empire.

A basic change, however, now occurred in government and society, as the Ch'in Legalist state was supplanted by a Confucianist state. This was because the class of landholders had become the leading power group. In the reign of Wu Ti (140-87 B.C.) they outlawed all learning except Confucianism and introduced civil service examinations based on Confucian classics for the recruitment of government officials. So in the Confucianist state under the Han a particular group, the landlord-scholar-official group, established itself as the ruling class. It set the fine tradition that learning and merit should be the criteria of leadership. It gave China many examples of good government. Nevertheless, being operated by people with vested interests, the Confucianist state also contained germs for abuse of power. In time the ruling class became insensitive to the needs of the masses and showed greater loyalty to its own group than to the state. For this reason we must differentiate between Confucianism and the Confucianist state. The former remained an inspiring force for the life of the people, while the latter emerged as an instrument of power for the privileged minority. Beginning with the Han, this type of control with minor variations characterized Chinese government until it was overthrown by the Communists in our own time.

The reign of Wu Ti, referred to above, was likewise a

period of imperial expansion. This aggressive emperor reaffirmed Han authority in South China and North Vietnam. Han armies conquered southern Manchuria and northern Korea. Three gigantic campaigns forced the Hsiung-nu (Huns) to retire beyond the Gobi desert. The diplomat-explorer Chang Ch'ien opened up the route across Sinkiang into Central Asia. Not only did trade develop along this international highway, with silk going to Asia Minor and grapes, alfalfa, and other articles coming in from Iran, but spheres of Chinese influence were staked out in Turkestan and Central Asia. Many Roman writers, such as Virgil, Horace, and Pliny the Elder, made references to China and Chinese products.

The maiden adventure of the Confucianist state touched off such an outburst of energy that the Han saw a Celestial Empire as the manifest destiny of China. Yet the landlord-scholar-officials were basically not interested in regions without agricultural wealth. They lamented the hardships of the frontier, considered trade a favour to the barbarian peoples, and regarded seeking their friendship as beneath China's dignity. If any conscious purpose existed, it was the desire of a vainglorious ruler to display Chinese power and brilliance. Thus the Han, having won an empire, never learned to hold it. This was a serious flaw in traditional imperial psychology which repeated itself in nearly all subsequent ages of greatness. Not until today has an end been put to it by the Communists, who have moved to exploit the industrial potential and geo-political advantages of these regions.

Internally the landlord-scholar-officials weakened the economy by exempting their own estates from taxation and making serfs of their tenants. This led Wang Mang, an imperial relative, to usurp the throne (9-23 A.D.) and to try land reform along socialist lines. As Wang failed the old order was reinstated (now called the Later Han), but the throne soon fell to weak or infant rulers. Bureaucratic corruption was compounded by factional strife. The eunuchs and the relatives of the dowager empresses fought one another for control, while the bureaucrats formed cliques, which joined first one side, then the other. This was the evil that brought about the collapse of the Confucianist state under the Han, as indeed it did under many subsequent dynasties.

We must not, however, let the sorrows of government blind us to the cultural and social progress under the Han. There was great activity in the field of letters. Scholars laboured hard to recover the Confucian classics lost under the Ch'in. Students were enrolled by the thousands in the College of Doctors. Ssu-ma Ch'ien and Pan Ku, like Herodotus and Thucydides, wrote their immortal histories. Pan Chao, an authoress, produced a guide to proper behaviour for women. A comprehensive dictionary of the Chinese language was compiled. With so much literary activity, men sought better ways to preserve their work. The brush pen was now widely used for writing. Then, in 105 A.D., a man in Hunan gave a tremendous stimulus to the spread of learning with his invention of paper made of hemp, rags, and mulberry bark. In the realm of philosophy and religion, Confucian orthodoxy led scholars to concentrate on the editing of old literature rather than on free thinking. In the Taoist school, the naturalistic philosophy of Lao-tzu gave way to a vulgarized system of rituals, prayers, and search for the elixir of life, to win the adherence of the illiterate masses.

During the four centuries of the Han population spread southward into the fertile Yangtze valley. Tea, originating in the south-east coastal area, became a national beverage. Under the Later Han, North Vietnam and Hainan Island were made a Chinese province, while the noted diplomats Pan Ch'ao and Kan Yin once again advanced

Chinese influence into Turkestan and Central Asia. Kan Yin even tried to establish contact with the Roman empire, although Chinese-Roman relations did not actually begin until a Roman envoy came to China in 166 A.D. Last but not least, direct contact between China and Japan was established in the first century A.D.

By the beginning of the third century the classical period of Chinese civilization—a period marked by the growth and maturing of a distinctive civilization under purely Chinese influences—drew to a close. The next eight hundred years brought cultural fusion, which absorbed outside forces but culminated in the blossoming and further extension of the classical civilization. This new cycle began with the collapse of the Han. The widespread poverty and unrest among the peasant masses towards the end of the Han erupted into revolts which opened the way for regional warlords to seize parts of the empire. At first there were three rival kingdoms, followed by the Chin which held unified control for a brief interval. Then nomad invaders from the north and west descended upon North China early in the fourth century and drove the Chin south of the Yangtze. From then until the midfifth century five barbarian stocks—two Turkic, one Tungusic (a Mongoloid race of Eastern Siberia and Manchuria), and two Tibetan—overran North China, setting up sixteen small states, while Chinese rule was confined to the territory south of the Yangtze under the exiled Chin régime. From 420-589 the division took the form of the Northern and Southern Dynasties: the Toba, a Turkic-Mongol power, ruled North China, while five successive Chinese military régimes ruled South China. So of the eight hundred years under consideration, the first half was an age of invasion and disunity. Not since the time of the Warring States were the people subjected to so much upheaval, dislocation, and suffering.

Yet an amazing process of cultural evolution and advance followed. As Chinese families from the north poured into the territory south of the Yangtze, the classical culture found new soil for accelerated growth. Bountiful harvests of rice stimulated population growth and supported a robust economy. Tea and silk enterprises prospered in the coastal regions, while the making of beautiful porcelain became big business in Kiangsi. A new and richer China thus arose in the south. Meantime, in North China the assimilative force of Chinese agricultural society made the actual and final conquest of the alien invaders. The intermingling of alien blood with Chinese blood created an invigorated race and society, but it reaffirmed the continuity of Chinese culture which, in its amplitude, unfailingly absorbed the newcomers.

One notable development—the spread of Buddhism—presented a more serious challenge to traditional Chinese civilization. Even so, the latter proved strong enough to hold its ground and to make use of Buddhism as it saw fit. A product of India, Buddhism taught men to renounce desire and to seek 'nirvana' or escape from repeated existences. Clearly this was a faith contrary to the humanistic and rationalistic traditions of the Chinese people. But in the particular form in which the religion was brought into China—Mahayana Buddhism—emphasis was placed on elements of wide mass appeal, such as repetitive prayers before bodhisattvas (idol-saints), which presumably would afford relief from misery if not actual guidance towards 'nirvana'. Accordingly, as invasions and wars caused widespread suffering in China, this religion gained tremendous popularity. Millions became ready converts. Buddhist temples were built throughout the country. An enormous volume of Buddhist literature was translated into Chinese. Yet nine out of ten Chinese converts to Buddhism were utilitarian: to them this was a handy ritual that might ease them through a time of hardship. For this reason Buddhism never dimmed the humanistic spirit of Chinese culture. Later, in the ninth and tenth centuries, it became the target of persecution. Its truly enduring effects were in the realm of art and architecture, since Buddhist temples, grottoes, statues, and pagodas definitely enriched Chinese art forms and motifs.

The undying vitality of Chinese civilization, which proved itself so dramatically in this prolonged upheaval, finally brought order out of chaos towards the end of the sixth century, and ushered in nearly four centuries of unification and strength under the Sui and T'ang dynasties. Like the Han following the Ch'in in the past, the T'ang was a direct successor of the short-lived Sui, so that they formed in effect an integral historical epoch. The factors that rallied the forces of reunification included land redistribution, which relieved agrarian distress; tax assessments which fixed varied levies in accordance with ability to pay; and a conscript army which drafted peasants from each prefecture. Furthermore, the Sui and the T'ang benefited from the new resources developed in the trans-Yangtze region. These circumstances set a broader and firmer stage for this era as compared with Han times. They greatly lowered public tension and consequently helped inaugurate a healthier and more successful Confucianist state.

Under the T'ang China was governed by benevolent despotism at its best. The emperors were assisted by ministers of the highest quality. They worked out a magnificent central government machinery which became the model for posterity. Three major divisions—one for policy making, a second for checking and supervision, and a third for the execution of policies—were created, ensuring a rational distribution of power. As for local government, China Proper was divided into ten Circuits (large provinces). Each Circuit was divided into Prefectures, which in turn were divided into Counties. From the capital Ch'ang-an, officials went forth to head these various levels of local government. Civil service examinations, based strictly on merit, became an inviolate institution. The censorate, with powers of impeachment, was introduced at this time. Of course, one must remember that this admirable system reached from the top to the county level only. But inasmuch as the traditional ideal was a Confucianist state, under which central control never touched the activities of the masses, the T'ang government may be considered as near perfection.

Under the Sui the old Grand Canal was built to link Hangchow (in Chekiang) with Loyang (in Honan). Chinese settled in Formosa and the Pescadores, and claimed the Liuchiu islands. This was some 900 years before Columbus and at a time when Japan was in the dim years of clan warfare. But the glory of empire reached its zenith under the T'ang. Its victories over the Turks (T'u-chüeh) cleared Sinkiang and Central Asia for the assertion of Chinese influence. The peoples of Sinkiang, Turkestan, Tibet, Bhutan, and Nepal recognized the suzerainty of China. These regions, together with Manchuria, Korea, Mongolia, and Vietnam, which likewise accepted Chinese control in varying degrees, formed a far-flung network of dependencies. Trans-continental routes led out from Kansu to India, Iraq, and Constantinople. Ch'ang-an was a truly cosmopolitan centre. To this great capital came Indians, Turks, Persians, Syrians, and other Arab nationals of the Middle East. Large numbers of Arabs and Persians, too, maintained a trading colony in Canton. The art of manufacturing paper was carried westward by the Arabs to the Near East and thence to Europe. Chinese seamen and traders for their part kept busy sea communications with South-East Asian countries.

Meantime, Chinese pilgrims went to India to study Buddhist scriptures, while Middle Eastern religions, such as Nestorian Christianity, Manichaeanism, Zoroastrianism, as well as Islam, found their way into China. The T'ang was tolerant of them, although towards the end of the dynasty a strong reaction set in which led to the banning of all alien faiths. Once again this showed the inherent nationalism of Chinese culture. In spite of all its cosmopolitanism the T'ang people resisted internationalism. Of interest in another direction was the continuous stream of Japanese students and envoys who visited Ch'ang-an to observe the Chinese government system and study Chinese literature and Buddhist teachings. This enabled them to launch reforms in Japan, which helped her to advance from clan sectionalism to a centralized government and society.

The T'ang was especially noted as a golden age of art and literature. Wu Tao-tzu set the form and tradition of figure painting. Three of China's greatest lyric poets—Li Po, Tu Fu, and Po Chü-i—flourished during this age. Their poetry tells of the beauties of the western countryside from which the three men came. Many of their themes touch on Taoist or Buddhist legends. One also learns about the brilliance and gaiety of the T'ang court, for all three men were favoured by the emperor during brief periods. Subtle, inspiring, and rich in imagery, the writings of T'ang poets are truly immortal. Since there was so much literary production, men sought easier ways to reproduce their works. Block printing, invented around 600, now came into wide use. In 868, the world's first printed book, the *Diamond Sutra*, was produced.

However, the T'ang, like the Han, suffered from the lack of a constructive imperial policy. Due to the usual indifference towards non-agricultural regions, the T'ang allowed its dependencies to remain under the control of their native leaders. When the T'ang army system collapsed in the mid-eighth century, Chinese governors bordering the subject lands openly made compacts with them and turned against the T'ang. Catastrophe overtook the dynasty in 755 when An Lu-shan, a typical border governor turned disloyal, revolted near Peking. He led a huge army southward, captured Loyang, and forced the T'ang emperor to flee from Ch'ang-an. The revolt was finally crushed, but only by using the aid of the Uighurs, a Turkic people from Sinkiang.

From this point on the fortunes of the T'ang declined rapidly. Regional officers turned independent satraps. The census and tax systems collapsed, leading to a single tax on land property alone. The eunuchs again became makers and breakers of emperors. A serious famine in Shantung in 880 touched off a peasant uprising which spread through most of the country. The T'ang ended its own rule when it begged for help from another subject people, the Shato Turks. During the half century following the end of the T'ang (907-960) North China came under a rapid alternation of Shato and Chinese governments, while South China was cut up into ten Chinese military régimes, until reunification was proclaimed by the founder of the Sung dynasty.

The founding of the Sung in 960 was an important landmark in Chinese history. Now we pass from the eight centuries of cultural fusion and blossoming of classical civilization into another long stretch of time—nine hundred years, from the mid-tenth century to the early nineteenth century—the keynote of which was the preservation of the traditional society and culture in the face of increased but ineffective challenges. During these centuries, covering the Sung, the Yüan, the Ming, and the early Ch'ing dynasties, which we shall now discuss, China's efforts were consumed in defending her spiritual heritage against mounting pressures which, however, were not powerful enough to undermine it.

The three hundred years of the Sung (960-1279) marked the weakest dynasty in Chinese history. To a certain extent the Sung rulers were not to blame for this weakness, because a shift in the population and economic structure of the country took place at this time. The Sung were unprepared for new problems. Up to now Ch'ang-an was China's centre of gravity, from which radiated control of the Yellow River plain to the east and the dependencies to the West. By the end of the eighth century, however, the centre of gravity had moved to the region between the lower courses of the Yangtze and Yellow rivers, as a result of the curtailed authority of government in Ch'ang-an, the growth of Central and South China, the transport facilities afforded by the Grand Canal, and the declining soil fertility in the north-west. Faced with the new situation, the Sung chose Kaifeng (in eastern Honan) as its capital, but the city enjoyed no commanding position with respect to either the nomads of the west or the powerful Tungusic tribes that had now arisen in the north-east. As a result in Ninghsia, in the north-west, a group of Tibetans, the Tanguts, set up an independent régime, Hsi Hsia, which defeated the Sung army and exacted annual tribute. The Khitans, a Tungusic people from Manchuria, maintained the powerful Liao dynasty, extended their control over the region between Peking and the Great Wall, and likewise exacted yearly tribute from the Sung. Later another Tungusic group, the Ju-chens, overthrew the Liao from its rear, set up the Chin dynasty, and posed an even greater threat to the integrity of China. Thus the northern perimeter of the Sung was completely exposed.

However, the Sung rulers had themselves to blame for the internal weakness of the régime. They paid huge pensions to powerful commanders whom they feared. They maintained a large army of hired mercenaries. A top-heavy bureaucracy ruled the country. In 1069-74 an outstanding ' New Dealer ', Wang An-shih, took steps to cut government expenditure and introduce agricultural credit, price control, and reforms in army, taxation, and education. But these measures aroused the ire of the landlord-scholar-officials and were dropped. In 1125 the Ju-chens drove south, took Kaifeng, and captured the Sung emperor together with his whole entourage. North China was now completely lost. A regional régime, known as the Southern Sung, carried on Chinese rule south of the Yangtze (1127-1279). Once again large numbers of Chinese families moved to the southern provinces. Once again these provinces experienced an economic boom. But no effective action was taken to recover North China. In the end the Mongols, a mixed people of Turkic and Tungusic origin from the borderlands of Manchuria and Mongolia, conquered the Chin in 1234 and the Southern Sung in 1279.

The response of the people to such political ineptitude was to seek scientific and cultural progress. The Chinese had always been inventive. But unless called upon by circumstances to act, they were slow to explore new fields of science or technology. Now, as maritime activities increased, the principle of magnetic polarity, known since Han times, was applied to the making of the mariner's compass. Likewise, the secret of explosives, known long before in assembling firecrackers, was now applied to the manufacture of hand-grenades and bombs. In agriculture cotton planting became popular in the Yangtze valley. Block printing of books, now widespread, led to extensive publication and dissemination of knowledge. In the making of porcelain the Sung potters had the true artist's eye for shape, while decorative effects were achieved by vivid glazes and by designs set in relief. But the acme of Sung art was landscape painting. Never too concerned with realistic detail, but absorbed in the timeless beauty of the landscape, the Sung painters were transcendentalists with a deep love of nature. Mountains, streams, wind, and mist were made to come alive by a few strokes of the utmost simplicity and suggestiveness. On the other hand, there was also an echo of decadence in Sung creativity. Candidates in civil service examinations parrotted the classical sayings without being tested for independent thinking. An unfortunate perversion of the sense of female beauty expressed itself in the practice of foot-binding.

In the field of philosophical speculation the Sung produced Neo-Confucianism. We may recall that Confucianism was a body of ethical teachings applicable to daily living. Since its supremacy was threatened by Buddhism with its cosmic explanations, the 'Sinophiles' of the Sung, especially their greatest thinker Chu Hsi, launched a drive to oust this alien influence. Chu borrowed extensively from Buddhism, and re-interpreted Confucianism by adding an ontological[1] coating to the original ethical[2] base. Chu's metaphysical theories were most elaborate. Yet the core of his thought rested on the interaction of Principle and Matter. When applied to government and social relationships, it insisted on following Principle; only in this way would Matter yield the greatest good. In effect, then, Neo-Confucianism was a Chinese 'counter-reformation' against Buddhism; it robbed Buddhism of its arguments and used them to confirm Confucian virtues. However, being conservative and nationalistic, it imposed narrow shackles on men's minds down to the nineteenth century.

[1] The branch of philosophy concerned with explaining the nature of things.

[2] The branch of philosophy concerned with right and wrong conduct.

Under the Mongol Yüan dynasty (1279-1368) the entire territory of China passed under alien rule. This was the climax of Chinese weakness begun under the Sung. But Kublai Khan and his successors remained in China only eighty-nine years, a very short time by China's calendar of events. Trying to resist assimilation, they ruled China by establishing four segregated classes: the Mongol masters as the privileged few; Central Asians as government personnel; the Chinese of North China with property but no political rights; and the Chinese of South China with no rights at all. This arrangement indeed discouraged assimilation, but also made it impossible for the Mongols to perpetuate their rule. Distrust and discrimination bred a fierce hatred of foreigners. The Yüan dynasty was ultimately toppled by Chinese nationalists amidst dissension over the succession. It is interesting to note that while in Russia the 'Tartar Yoke' bequeathed to the Muscovites a tyrannical absolutism, China's civilization kept its poise and emerged unaffected by the whirlwind conquest of the Khans. This was the best commentary on the nature of the Mongol challenge: powerful, but not strong enough to undermine China's traditional society and culture.

If anything the Chinese had the better of the Mongols. The Khan made Peking the capital *par excellence*. Known as Khan Baliq (city of the Khan; hence Cambaluc), Peking now took the place of Ch'ang-an as the leading metropolis of China. The Yüan built a new Grand Canal, branching off from the old Grand Canal at the Hwai intersection and leading due north to Tientsin. It also consolidated control over Yunnan, bordering Burma. In maritime expansion, its invasions of Japan ended in disaster, but the expeditions to Java were successful.

Westward, trans-continental highways were once again kept open. The use of gunpowder and the improved art of printing spread to Europe, while missionaries brought a variety of religions into China. Roman Catholicism enjoyed favour for a brief period. Islam was re-introduced and took root in the north-west and in Yunnan. Lamaism, the Tibetan version of Buddhism, was embraced by the Mongols and has persisted among them ever since. This was the age in which Marco Polo made his celebrated travels to China. His book was the first eye-witness report of China's power and splendour. Last but not least, this was the golden age of Chinese drama. With the vernacular in vogue and the doors of officialdom closed to Chinese scholars, many of them turned their talents to play-writing. To this day Yüan plays are among the most treasured masterpieces in Chinese dramatic literature.

Under the Ming dynasty (1368-1644) Chinese nationalism staged a powerful come-back. Vaunted sentiments of national pride and triumph coloured every aspect of public life. The Confucianist state was re-established, with the landlord-scholar-officials in power. Except for a short period Peking remained the permanent capital. At the height of its power the Ming held a large empire, extending from Korea to Vietnam. Yet Sinkiang, Tibet, and Mongolia were beyond its control. On the other hand, Manchuria came under Ming dominion.

The Ming also developed a navy, which in the first half of the fifteenth century sent out a series of expeditions to the South Seas. The name of China as a sea power was carried to the Indonesian islands, to Thailand, India and Ceylon, and further west to the Persian Gulf and east Africa. But these voyages were prompted by a desire to track down a pretender to the throne. Once that issue was dead, the sea ventures were called off. Thus China ceased to be a sea power almost as quickly as she had become one. This is significant because just when the Ming gave up sea-faring ventures, the South Seas were penetrated by the Europeans. We shall discuss this in a later connection. Suffice it to note here that as the successive groups of Europeans (first the Portuguese, then the Spaniards and the Dutch, and finally the English) arrived on the Chinese coast, they found China committed to isolation and without sea power. By the middle of the sixteenth century China did not even have ships enough to maintain her coastal defences. Japan, hitherto a neighbour of little consequence, now harrassed the Chinese coast with plundering raids, while her redoubtable general Hideyoshi made devastating invasions of Korea. Although the Japanese were repulsed, the war over Korea might have brought serious consequences for the Ming but for the death of Hideyoshi in 1598.

In a real sense the Ming was the first dynasty to show the ageing of traditional Chinese civilization. While the régime rose on the crest of a growing nationalism, it failed to take the initiative in introducing timely reforms of any kind. Unlike the benevolent despots of the T'ang, the Ming rulers were unreasonable and cruel. High officials often faced the bastinado[1] in court. Criticisms of the government were taboo, and large numbers of eunuchs were employed as imperial spies. Political oppression led to intellectual sterility. To be sure, many books, especially encyclopædias, were published under the Ming. The great idealist philosopher Wang Yang-ming was a towering figure in the early sixteenth century. But the rank and file of educated people were blanketed by an atmosphere of stagnation. Under the system of the 'Eight Legged Essay', candidates in civil service examinations were required to write essays in eight parallel paragraphs and in a prescribed number of words as though Confucius were speaking rather than to express themselves. This type of test,

---

[1] Beating with a stick on the soles of the feet.

which persisted into the twentieth century, seriously limited the thinking of scholars.

Towards the close of the dynasty power fell into the hands of insolent eunuchs. The group that suffered most was the peasant masses. Following a round of famines and agrarian outbreaks, two peasant armies arose in the northwest and in the upper Yangtze valley. The Ming government was too demoralized to cope with them. When the rebellious forces marched on Peking in 1644 the Ming emperor committed suicide, leaving the country prostrate. No Chinese group was able to restore order. Instead, one Chinese general, driven by personal hatred, opened the way to Peking to a military power that had arisen in Manchuria. The outcome was that another alien group, this time the Manchus, a Tungusic people of Manchuria, imposed its rule on the Chinese.

Like the Mongols, the Manchus extended their control over all China. But unlike the Mongols, the Manchu rule lasted from 1644 till the Revolution of 1911. During the first half of the dynasty history repeated itself, as the Manchus made military conquest of China and China made cultural conquest of the Manchus. Thus until about 1820 the traditional society and culture flourished, marking the last phase of the nine hundred years of maintenance of the old order. The Manchu emperors of this period, among the greatest in history, governed the country with strength and sagacity. While guarding their prerogatives, they ruled like Chinese monarchs and used Chinese officials and institutions. They gave the country peace and prosperity. Great works were produced in literature, art, and history. The frontiers of the empire extended even farther than those of earlier ages. In the north they embraced Mongolia; in the east Formosa was taken and Korea recognized Chinese suzerainty, as did the Liuchiu islands. Westward not only was Sinkiang brought into the empire, but Chinese dominion extended beyond the Pamir Mountains. Across the southern borders vassal status was accepted by Burma, Thailand, and Vietnam. China was then the mightiest and wealthiest empire in the world.

During this period the Europeans trading along the Chinese coast regarded the Manchu government with great respect, although they vainly hoped to remove Chinese restrictions and widen their trading opportunities. Just as the Portuguese were the leading Europeans in the Ming period, the English forged ahead as the principal traders under the Manchus. The first English ships arrived in Canton in 1637, while the English East India Company entered the field in 1699. From the standpoint of cultural interchange this was the heyday of the Jesuit missionaries. As evangelists of Christianity they encountered great difficulties. But as devotees of learning they exerted tremendous influence. Through them China acquired Western knowledge of geography, astronomy, and mathematics, while Europe learned about Chinese philosophy, customs, arts and crafts. There grew up in Europe at this time a fashion in things Chinese. Homes had Chinese rooms and rock gardens. Smart ladies rode about in sedan chairs and toyed with Chinese fans. Even the philosophers, Voltaire among them, thought that they had found a utopia when they learned of Chinese ideas on government and education.

As China entered the nineteenth century the grandeur of empire continued intact on the surface, but powerful and uncompromising forces set in to take the old order apart. For this reason, we must deal at greater length with the hundred years from the eighteen-forties to the nineteen-forties. This part of our story is the vital link between the waning of traditional China and the rise of the new China under Communism.

One of the major forces that shook the foundations of the Manchu empire was the sharp increase of population without a corresponding increase in agricultural production. From 1644 to 1700 the population fluctuated between 100 and 120 million. By 1795 it reached 275 million, and by 1850 it passed the 400 million mark. However, land under cultivation, estimated at 7½ million *ching* (a *ching* roughly equals 15 acres) in 1701, was not more than 10 million *ching* in 1850. Such a situation had never happened before. In the past misrule had indeed led to peasant revolts, such as those at the end of the Han, the T'ang, and the Ming. But with population below 100 million and landholding per head tolerably comfortable, no agrarian unrest remained insoluble once measures were taken to restore the health of the Confucianist state. Now, however, population pressure on the land was heavy. The sharp decrease in landholding per head reduced millions of peasants to a bare subsistence and sent many into debt to absentee landlords. These great numbers of landless peasants had been China's most pressing problem ever since the opening of the nineteenth century.

Throughout the first half of the century peasant uprisings of major proportions rocked the north, the north-west, and the south-west, sparing only the rich provinces south of the Yangtze. However, in 1850-65 the worst of all uprisings engulfed this agricultural heartland of the country. The Taiping Rebellion arose out of agrarian distress in Kwangsi plus an admixture of religion, for the rebel leader Hung Hsiu-ch'üan claimed to be the brother of Jesus. As the revolt spread northward to the Yangtze valley and thence eastward to the delta region, it acquired tremendous momentum by spreading propaganda against the Manchus and applying semi-Communistic practices. Hung and his associates of course could not have read Karl Marx; but they hit upon a programme which called for land redistribution, communal property, brotherhood of all classes, and equality of the sexes. In practice they could not enforce true land redistribution on account of the war. But the tillers were given the land under cultivation, and rent to landlords was abolished. This aroused so much enthusiasm among the peasant masses that wherever the rebels went they were able to recruit fresh army units and organize women's auxiliary brigades.

The rebel movement carried nine provinces and established a new government in Nanking. But the Taipings were extremely destructive. Loss in lives reached twenty million. They had no programme for a sound economy. And, in spite of the military talent of their generals, internal dissension destroyed the leadership in Nanking. The rebellion was finally put down not by the Manchu army, but by volunteers raised by the Chinese gentry class led by Tseng Kuo-fan, with the help of the 'Ever-Victorious Army' under Captain (later General) Charles Gordon. When the holocaust ended in 1865 a few things became clear. The Manchu dynasty was in the doldrums. Its bankruptcy, however, was obscured by the rise of the Chinese gentry in defence of the old order. Thus the conservative group continued in power without introducing effective reforms. As for the masses, their situation became progressively worse since their needs were not met. But an important fact had been demonstrated, namely that peasant discontent represented a great reservoir of revolutionary power.

The second powerful force that engulfed the Manchu empire was Western imperialism. We have noted that in the early phases of foreign trade in Canton the Europeans vainly hoped to ease the restrictions imposed by the Chinese authorities. But as trade grew and the trading colony expanded the sources of friction between the Europeans and the Chinese multiplied. Great Britain sent two missions to Peking to negotiate for normal relations, but failed completely. In 1834, as the charter of the English East India Company ended, an official of the British government rather than a Company representative came to Canton to handle Britain's relations with China. Tension quickly mounted. Anglo-Chinese differences became irreconcilable. Specifically, British grievances centred on China's trade restrictions, her refusal to treat Britain as an equal, the conflicting legal procedures, and the importation of opium. Underlying these specific issues there was the irrepressible clash between Western expansionism and Chinese seclusion, between Western superiority and Chinese inferiority in technology and organization.

In the ensuing war, commonly known as the Opium War (1839-41), China was decisively defeated by Great Britain. Now she opened ports for foreign trade, ceded Hong Kong as a British colony, paid a large war indemnity, consented to a customs tariff fixed by treaty, granted extra-territoriality (the right of British consular officials to try British subjects in China), and subscribed to the most-favoured-nation clause, which guaranteed Britain all further rights which China might grant to any other power. This was the beginning of the unequal treaties, a long series of crippling blows at China's sovereignty which acted like a vice strangling China.

If China held any illusions that the Europeans would submit to her civilizing influence as had her historical invaders, these illusions were dispelled by the events of the second half of the nineteenth century. Following on the heels of the British came the Americans and the French, who obtained treaties similar to the one ending the Opium War. After a decade of fresh complications, Britain and France won another war against China. This time the foreign powers obtained additional privileges, such as the cession of Kowloon to Britain, increased indemnities, opening of more trade ports, residence of diplomatic representatives in Peking, opening of the Yangtze to foreign navigation and commerce, legalization of the coolie trade (tricking Chinese peasants into forced labour overseas) and of the importation of opium, the right for foreigners to travel in the interior of China, and toleration of missionaries throughout the country.

While the maritime powers made these inroads Russia, who had had trade relations across the Siberian border for two centuries, likewise brought pressure to bear on China's northern perimeter. She took the Blagoveshchensk region on the northern bank of the Amur river in 1858, and the Vladivostok region east of the Ussuri river in 1860. In the three ensuing decades the powers maintained a solid front to hold China to her treaty obligations and used every possible opportunity to extend foreign economic control. Russia, taking advantage of the Muslim rebellion in Sinkiang, penetrated into the Ili valley. In more distant corners of the empire Burma and Vietnam passed under the control of Britain and France respectively.

In the years 1894-99 China's fortunes sank to a new low level when she was threatened with partition. The vicious circle began with Japan's defeat of China in the war of 1894-95 over Korea. By the Treaty of Shimonoseki China recognized the independence of Korea; ceded Formosa, the Pescadores, and the Liaotung Peninsula (off southern Manchuria) to Japan; agreed to a huge war indemnity of 300 million taels (a tael equals nearly three shillings); and granted Japan extra-territoriality and the most-favoured-nation treatment. In China's plight Russia stepped forth to proffer help. She forced Japan to return the Liaotung Peninsula to China and then turned to seek rewards for herself. A secret treaty with China in 1896 gave her important railway rights in North Manchuria. Another treaty in 1898 enabled her to lease the naval base of Port

Arthur and the port of Dairen from China, thus bringing Russia penetration into the Liaotung Peninsula itself.

Russia's far-flung ambitions immediately led the other powers to seek similar concessions from China. The notorious scramble in 1898 for loans, leaseholds, and agreements on spheres of interest marked the nadir of China's fortunes. Britain leased Weihaiwei, on the Shantung peninsula, as a naval base. In addition she obtained the leased territory in Kowloon, and made the Yangtze valley her sphere of interest. Germany leased Kiaochow Bay as her naval base, including the port of Tsingtao, and obtained railway and other concessions in Shantung. France, on her part, leased Kwangchow Bay in South China, plus railway and mining concessions in Yunnan. The last act in this scramble was the agreement with Japan whereby China promised 'not to alienate' Fukien province from Japan's influence. At this point the United States entered the mêlée with the Open Door policy. This was, in fact, a protest against the various spheres of interest and a reiteration of the principle of equal commercial opportunity. Its purpose was to safeguard American treaty rights in China rather than to champion China's recovery of her lost rights.

Such mounting crises convinced every thinking man in China that modern imperialism was an implacable foe. The tragedy lay in China's inability to find an effective answer to the challenge. While the battle for concessions was going on, a reform movement broke out in Peking. The young emperor Kuang Hsu, aided by progressive scholars like K'ang Yu-wei and Liang Ch'i-ch'ao, issued a series of edicts in the summer of 1898 ordering reforms in government, education, and in the military system. But the 'Hundred Days of Reform' came quickly to an end. Not only did it lack popular support, but the arch-conservative Empress Dowager T'zu-hsi staged a *coup d'état*.

She imprisoned the young emperor, rescinded the reform edicts, and installed an ultra-reactionary régime with herself at the helm.

Uninformed and bigoted, her Imperial Majesty proceeded to find her own solution by endorsing a fanatical anti-foreign outbreak, the Boxer Uprising, which brought about an even greater crisis for China. The Boxers, made up of secret societies and local militia, murdered foreign missionaries and destroyed their property in many parts of North China. With a nod of approval from the Court, they moved on Peking early in 1900 to attack the Legation Quarter, to 'slaughter the foreigners and save the dynasty'. When the Boxers repulsed an expedition led by Admiral Seymour (June 1900), they were emboldened to murder the German minister and a counsellor of the Japanese Legation. Now the Manchu Court brought down the wrath of all interested powers. An Allied expedition marched on Peking. The Boxers proved helpless. The siege of the Legations was lifted, and the Imperial Court fled to Sian (August 1900). The mad anti-foreign drive had ended in total disaster. The Boxer Protocol (1901) imposed severe punitive terms, such as punishment of responsible officials, fortification of the Legation Quarter, stationing of foreign troops to guard the road to Peking, and above all an indemnity of 450 million taels. If any doubt existed about the bankruptcy of the Manchu government, it vanished following the Boxer catastrophe.

One thing after another furnished proof that national disaster would be a certainty under continued Manchu leadership. There was humiliation and bewilderment at the end of the Russo-Japanese War (1904-05), when China was forced to recognize Japanese gains in Manchuria. The Empress Dowager's promise of constitutional monarchy struck the people as an empty gesture. In 1908 both the Empress Dowager and the reform emperor Kuang Hsu died, leaving even more mediocre leaders in control. When the provincial assemblies met in 1909 and the national assembly in 1910, the deputies were in an intransigent mood. The country was on the verge of revolution.

The overthrow of the Manchu dynasty and the founding of the Chinese Republic (1911-12) were inseparably linked with the name of Sun Yat-sen, the father of the Chinese revolution. Born in 1866 in Chungshan (near Canton), Sun received a Western as well as a Chinese education, practised medicine for a brief period, but became actively engaged in anti-Manchu conspiracies in the early eighteen-nineties. At one point he found it necessary to flee the country. He proceeded to Hawaii and America to organize Chinese groups abroad for revolution. From the beginning Sun repudiated constitutional monarchy and advocated the establishment of a republic. His revolutionary headquarters were based in Japan, but he travelled far and wide to enlist support. Once when in England he fell into the hands of kidnappers belonging to the Chinese Legation, but was released upon the intervention of Lord Salisbury.

Sun founded the first revolutionary party, the 'Revive China Society', in 1895. Ten years later he replaced it with the 'Common Alliance League', with increased membership and a systematized programme, which in later years grew into the *San Min Chu I* ('Three People's Principles'). At this time, however, Sun's emphasis was on the overthrow of the Manchu dynasty. This fitted well the growing trend towards revolution. Accordingly, Sun's followers carried out insurrections in many parts of the country. After a number of abortive attempts the uprising in Wuchang on October 10, 1911 finally crowned the revolution with success, and the Chinese Republic was born. The Manchu emperor abdicated. Sun was made President of the Provisional Government in Nanking.

Unfortunately the Republic failed to lead a healthy life. Except for a dedicated few, Sun's party, known now as the Kuomintang (National People's Party), was weighted down with opportunists neither able nor prepared to fight for democracy. Power in North China fell into the hands of Yüan Shih-kai, the strong man of the old régime and now the senior of a group of warlords known as the Pei-yang generals, who had no love for republican principles. By a series of manœuvres Yüan took over the Presidency, moved the government back to Peking, and proceeded to strangle the infant Republic. By 1914, when Yüan introduced a new constitution to give enlarged powers to himself, Sun and the Kuomintang had been virtually eliminated from power.

In 1915 Yüan's supporters promoted a movement to reinstate the monarchy with Yüan as emperor. The moment for this daring move, however, was badly chosen. For in the winter of 1914-15 Yüan submitted abjectly to Japan's bid for hegemony over China. Taking advantage of the First World War, Japan occupied Shantung in the autumn of 1914, and then presented the notorious Twenty-one Demands to Yüan in January 1915. These Demands asked for ex-German rights in Shantung, increased Japanese control in Manchuria and Mongolia, Japanese monopoly of iron and coal industries in the Yangtze valley, non-alienation of territory to other powers, plus administrative, military, and economic provisions that would have made China a Japanese protectorate. After a period of fear and procrastination Yüan accepted nearly all of these Demands. Such a cloud of gloom descended upon the nation that May 9, the day on which he capitulated to the Japanese ultimatum, became known in history as 'National Humiliation Day'. Against this unfortunate background the monarchist movement was thoroughly discredited. Public anger and the revolt of the south-western provinces forced the cancellation of the scheme. To Yüan it was a death blow. In June 1916 his life came to an unexpected and dramatic end.

The period of Yüan Shih-kai exposed the utter inadequacy of the Confucianist state for coping with the problems of twentieth century China. The paramount task before the nation was to face up to the economic and social needs of the masses and the pressures created by foreign imperialism. However, more trying years were to intervene before this could take place. After Yüan's death things became worse under Premier T'uan Ch'i-jui, another Peiyang warlord. Bent on military dictatorship, T'uan declared war on Germany. His worst act was signing away Chinese rights in Shantung in secret agreements with Japan. These traitorous promises contributed directly to China's defeat at the Versailles Conference. This time the Chinese people reacted with positive demonstrations of strength. In the famous May 4 (1919) movement, angry crowds attacked T'uan's cabinet ministers, called a nationwide boycott of Japanese goods, and brought T'uan's government to an ignominious end. This marked the birth of militant nationalism in contemporary China. Henceforth the by-word for patriotic endeavour was 'to overthrow the warlords internally and the imperialists externally'.

The May 4 movement unleashed many progressive forces. True, another decade of civil war ravaged the country. True, China lost her control over Mongolia and Tibet. True, on the diplomatic front, the Washington Conference (1921-22) paid lip service to respecting Chinese sovereignty, but refused to abolish extra-territoriality or grant tariff autonomy. Nonetheless, the national awakening of 1919 set powerful forces in motion. Chinese intellectuals launched a drive to put science and materialism above Confucian moral philosophy. This 'emancipation' movement was carried on by two groups. The admirers of

American-type pragmatism and liberalism advocated democracy, science, and modern education. Starting by popularizing the vernacular in preference to the classical style of writing, they launched a new literary movement which led to attacks on the ideas and customs of the traditional society. The other group, much smaller and inspired by the Bolshevik Revolution, joined the battle but contended that Marxism, not democracy, was the panacea for China. This great intellectual ferment was responsible for mobilizing the Chinese people to press for the overthrow of the warlords and of the imperialists.

For this new struggle the people again turned to Sun Yat-sen, who since 1917 had maintained a revolutionary foothold in Canton, urging a punitive expedition (or 'Northern Expedition' as he called it) to end the anarchy in the north. By this time Sun had put his revolutionary doctrines, the *San Min Chu I*, in final form. He called for a free and independent China, stressing the abolition of the unequal treaties. He urged democracy, and spelled out the people's rights as well as the government's powers. In his economic programme he emphasized the state's role in solving the problems of food, clothing, shelter, and travel, urged 'land to the cultivator' to relieve agrarian distress, and favoured the development of state capital in industry. Sun believed that revolution and reconstruction should proceed by three stages: first, by military rule; second, by political tutelage; and last, by constitutional government.

Having formulated his programme, Sun however found no sympathy among the foreign powers. Soviet Russia was the only nation willing to extend a helping hand. Accordingly, in 1923 he reached an understanding with Moscow, and undertook the historic reorganization of the Kuomintang in 1924. This was an event of great importance, because it helped to end the anarchy of the warlords, to release the flood tides of nationalism, to usher in Kuomintang rule, and above all to bring forward Communism as a paramount issue.

Sun was convinced that radical measures were needed to put teeth into the Nationalist Revolution. For this reason the Kuomintang was reformed with tight discipline and strong organization. Revolutionary strategy was mapped out with Soviet advisers, led by Michael Borodin. Meantime Sun looked with approval upon the members of the Chinese Communist Party, which had been founded three years earlier, in 1921, by the radical intellectuals of the May 4 movement. They were admitted into the Kuomintang to collaborate in the revolutionary work. To win popular support a policy of mass organization was adopted, stressing the formation of peasant and labour unions. Finally, a revolutionary army was created, headed by a young officer, Chiang Kai-shek. These measures immediately injected new life into the revolutionary régime in Canton.

Unfortunately in March 1925 Sun died of cancer, amidst nation-wide mourning. Despite the loss the Nationalist Revolution went on apace. Canton became the hub of revolutionary activities. Anti-imperialist crusades soon broke out in Shanghai and Shameen to herald the advent of the revolutionary tide. However, a rift now developed over the question of cooperation with the Communists and the Comintern. Wang Ching-wei and the Kuomintang Left, who were closest to the thinking of Sun, urged continued cooperation with the Communists and Soviet advisers, with broad economic and social reforms rather than Communism as their goal. Holding the other end of the argument was the Kuomintang Right, who wanted to oust all the Communists and end the two-party collaboration. In the Centre was Chiang Kai-shek, who until the early part of 1926 supported Wang's position, chiefly because he regarded Communist and Soviet help as essential to the successful launching of the Northern Expedition.

Shortly afterwards, however, Chiang's position changed. Accepting the support and advice of powerful financial groups in Shanghai, he began to urge the conquest of the rich south-eastern provinces as the first phase of the Northern Expedition. In Chiang's calculation these provinces would give him a decided advantage over all other groups around him. Thus began his differences with the Communists and the Kuomintang Left. With the army behind him, Chiang prevailed. The revolutionary forces began their northward drive in July 1926. In September they took the Wuhan cities in the mid-Yangtze valley. Then they turned eastward, capturing the south-eastern provinces until Shanghai and Nanking fell early in 1927. As expected, this broadening of revolutionary territory changed the situation in Chiang's favour. Assured of the resources of this area, he no longer needed Communist support. As a result, he set up a new régime in Nanking in open defiance of the Left and the Communists, who had moved the Canton government to Wuhan.

The Wuhan government indeed enjoyed constitutional legitimacy, but controlled only two provinces, lacked internal unity, and depended on armies of dubious loyalty. Moreover, the Communist-directed labour strikes alienated the public, while the Comintern had no real intention of upholding the Kuomintang Left. In contrast, Chiang Kai-shek now controlled at least five rich provinces. His armies were large, loyal, and unified. The support of the bankers, merchants, and landlords was assured. His turn to the Right also won him the support of the Kuomintang conservatives and of the Western powers. After his new government was set up in Nanking in April 1927, he immediately carried out large-scale arrests of the Communists and executions of workers.

The passions of the time were such that Chiang now carried his anti-Communist and anti-Left policy to excess. Allied with financiers, landlords, and party reactionaries, he neglected economic and social reforms, which were after all what China needed most. From this point on his political philosophy showed the strong influence of the traditional Confucianist state. Chiang sought unification through military and political power. Under his protection the landlord-scholar-officials, presuming an inherent right to rule, dug in to strengthen the bureaucracy, but gave no thought to necessary changes. Thus the gap between the government and the masses, which was closed in 1924-26, was again widened, and the bracing spirit of Canton was buried under the murky skies of Shanghai and Nanking. Yet the tragedy of the Nationalist Revolution was such that the acts of the Communists in Wuhan played directly into the hands of Chiang. In June 1927, when it was made public that the Comintern sought the total overthrow of the Kuomintang, the political life of Wang Ching-wei and the Kuomintang Left was doomed. The one hope of realizing the original programme of Sun Yat-sen, which was liberal socialism by peaceful means, was lost for good. Now the Communists went underground, while Chiang's power became supreme.

The first decade of the Nationalist Government in Nanking (1928-37) was marked by a visible increase in the authority of the régime and in economic progress. Most of the Pei-yang warlords had disappeared from the national scene. The National Economic Council promoted reconstruction, especially in the development of communications, industries, and natural resources. Education made remarkable progress, as new schools and universities were established with generous government support. Foreign trade, mainly with Britain, Japan, and the United States, multiplied in volume. The government not only received diplomatic recognition from most of the nations, but made tariff autonomy a reality. To be sure, foreign infringements of Chinese sovereignty persisted, and foreign capital investments with foreign control continued to dominate the economic and financial scene. But in all fairness it must be said that China faced a greater promise of peace and prosperity than she had at any time since the founding of the Republic. This was not unlike the initial years of prosperity that marked the traditional dynasties.

Such outward vigour, however, was deceptive. Chiang Kai-shek's methods, representing traditional statecraft of the highest order, failed to work under the conditions of the nineteen-thirties. Thus, having pushed the Northern Expedition to formal completion over North China, he introduced the period of political tutelage, under which no opposition to the Kuomintang was permitted. He also concentrated all power in himself by heading the army, the party, and the government at one and the same time. But before long difficulties set in. First he became involved in costly civil wars with dissenting generals in the south and north-west. Then he made compromises with Marshal Chang of Manchuria to obtain a nominal allegiance. The furore over a Provisional Constitution, which transferred large powers from the party central committee to the president of the Nationalist Government, brought him into head-on collision with veteran party leaders, who seceded from Nanking and launched a rebel régime in Canton (1931).

Now we must turn to the rejuvenation of the Com-

3. *The People's Assembly Hall, Peking.* Built in eleven months for the tenth anniversary of the Chinese People's Republic (1959). It seats 10,000 people, and is used for operas and concerts as well as for political meetings.

4. *Nomadic peoples of the border lands.* Mongols of the Great Steppe, showing the round felt houses they have used for at least two thousand years, and the horses they have ridden on their famous migrations and conquests.

5

munist movement during these years. After their defeat in 1927, a new group of Communist leaders proceeded to seize the revolutionary initiative from Chiang Kai-shek. The man who gave direction to this group was Mao Tse-tung. Son of a farming family in Hunan, Mao had a university education, knew Chinese history by heart, and was a firm believer in Marxism-Leninism. He was one of the founding members of the Chinese Communist Party, and had participated in revolutionary work in Canton and Wuhan. Unlike most of his comrades, however, Mao was a realist who had independent convictions plus a capacity to fight for those convictions. These qualities now combined to make him the man of the hour.

Mao held that the Communist Party needed an independent base, an independent government, and an independent army. To achieve these objectives, the Party should ignore Comintern orders, abandon city uprisings, and organize the peasant masses, whose need for reforms furnished an unlimited source of revolutionary strength. He believed that by combining the lessons of Chinese peasant revolts with Marxism-Leninism, the Chinese Communists could launch an irresistible revolution. He rallied around him Chu Teh, Chou En-lai, and other comrades of the same mind. In 1928 they developed the first peasant revolutionary base on the Hunan-Kiangsi border. Soon a string of Chinese soviets spread eastward through Kiangsi into Fukien. In 1931 the Chinese Soviet Republic was established with Jui-chin as its capital. Everywhere they went Mao's group organized the landless peasants, by overthrowing the landlords and redistributing their

5. *Agriculture.* Plenty of people, shortage of machinery, and awkward sites keep hand labour well to the fore in Chinese agriculture. These Commune-members are watering fruit-trees on a steep hillside which they have recently terraced and planted.
6. *Ploughing, old and new.* Wooden ploughs drawn by oxen, and multiple steel ploughs drawn by powerful tractors.

land to the peasants. With mass enthusiasm aroused, they taught the peasants how to set up village soviets to govern the countryside. Labour brigades were organized; group farming was introduced; a Red Army was created; and guerilla warfare was taught as a means of both offence and defence. For the first time in Chinese history, control by the central government really reached the masses.

The 'Mao Tse-tung line' was a departure from the orthodox Communist doctrine, which maintained that revolution should be based on an urban proletariat. But Mao was a master, not a slave, of revolutionary doctrines. The realism of his thinking led him to urge peasant revolution to fit the conditions of China. Mao never eschewed orthodox Communism. But holding that there was a right place and a right time for everything, he had to deviate before he could conform. The implementation of this indigenous version of Communist revolution gave Mao and his group a distinct sense of independence from the Kremlin.

The battle lines were thus drawn between Chiang and the Kuomintang on the one hand, and Mao and the Communists on the other. But the situation was complicated by the Japanese invasion of Manchuria in September 1931. The Kuomintang government, unable to check Japan's aggression, pursued an appeasement policy, which however strengthened the hands of its enemies. A vicious circle of crises and repercussions made Chiang's position most difficult. Following the loss of the Manchurian provinces and the failure of the League of Nations to do anything concrete to stop Japan, the invader moved closer to Peking, forcing Chiang to sign the Tangku Truce, the 'Munich Agreement of North China'. Anti-Japanese sentiment enveloped the whole country, punctuated by popular demands for resistance.

Chiang was of course fully aware of his difficult situation. But he demanded 'unification before resistance'. His programme was to placate the Japanese so long as they did not take Peking and to 'wipe out' the Communists in the meantime. But Chiang's army, accustomed to positional warfare, hit a stone wall when confronted with the guerrilla forces of Mao Tse-tung. Chiang's six anti-Communist campaigns failed to dislodge the Communists. Only the use of a blockade forced them to flee to Yen-an, in northern Shensi, on the famous Long March (1934-35). Even this was a Pyrrhic victory, for the peasant masses in Central China never regained confidence in the Kuomintang government.

After the Communists re-established themselves in Yen-an they won wide public support with a moderate revolutionary programme, and for propaganda purposes called for 'resistance above civil war'. Their demand for a united front against Japanese aggression was rejected by Chiang. But the troops sent by Chiang for the drive on Yen-an fell convert to the Communist propaganda. Following a truce between the Communists and these troops, Chiang Kai-shek was taken captive in a sensational coup in Sian in December 1936. Chiang was released by his captors, but only after the decision was made to end his war against the Communists and to fight an all-out war against the Japanese. This marked a decisive turning point. It not only meant a new lease of life for the Communists; but by committing himself to war against Japan, Chiang faced the grim prospect of losing his military power altogether.

The war against Japan broke out in July 1937. Japan quickly took Peking and Tientsin and swept southward into the North China provinces. In Shansi the enemy advance was halted by the Communist Eighth Route Army. But in August the war spread to Shanghai, which became the theatre of major fighting. Here the main body

of Chiang's army was thrown into three months of bloody
battle until it was largely destroyed. Nanking was lost in
December 1937, followed by the fall of Hankow and Canton in October 1938. Chiang moved the government to
Chunking, fourteen hundred miles up the Yangtze from
the sea, to continue resistance. Large numbers of government workers, as well as factories and schools, went west
with him. This was not unlike the historic migrations
from North China, when thousands fled before the nomad
invaders. But this time the south-west was not an area of
booming prosperity, while the seaboard provinces in the
east, which formed the pillars of Kuomintang strength,
were lost to Japan.

Starting from 1939 a stalemate set in. There were now
three Chinas: Occupied China under Japan in the east;
Red China under the Communists in the north-west; and
Kuomintang China under Chiang in the south-west. Japan
made few further gains of territory against either Red
China or Kuomintang China. Chiang stuck doggedly to
a policy of 'trading space for time', but was unable to
recover any lost territory. The Communist forces of Red
China, however, were more aggressive. As Japanese occupation was confined to cities and railway lines, the Communists extended their control behind the Japanese lines
by making use of guerilla units.

This disparity in the power of Red China and of Kuomintang China became the keynote of all subsequent
developments. Mao Tse-tung's revolutionary strategy now
began to prove its worth, thanks in part to its intrinsic
strength, in part to the military and social upheaval caused
by the war. While Chiang's prestige remained high as he
rejected Japan's repeated peace overtures, the difficulties
besetting his government were insurmountable. Without
the resources of the seaboard provinces, production fell
and the war effort faltered. He relied on Szechwan land-

lords and other conservative groups, thus moving further away from social reforms. In time the more rapacious persons in his government engaged in speculation and profiteering which, together with the mounting inflation, all but ruined the economy. By contrast the Communists thrived on the exigencies of the war. Taking advantage of social dislocation and population migration, they carried out a dynamic social transformation behind the enemy lines, first in North China, then in the lower Yangtze region and in Manchuria. They penetrated into new areas by guerrilla warfare, won mass support by land reform, and controlled the local governments by setting up coalition régimes under Communist leadership. For the first time in Chinese history the traditional society was not only upset by mass unrest amidst invasion and war, but it was driven into a dead end by the rise of a new social order which the Communists had devised to enlist the allegiance of the people.

The Kuomintang-Communist united front against Japan now began to fall apart. Alarmed by the expansion of Communist power, Chunking re-opened the civil war. Undaunted, Mao Tse-tung demanded that the Kuomintang dictatorship should be ended and a coalition government created in its place. When China became an ally of Britain and the United States in the Pacific War (December 1941), the Communist Party and the Red Army were already well entrenched in Occupied China, with 'Liberated Areas' (areas under Communist control) spread across North China, Manchuria, and large parts of the eastern seaboard provinces. Chiang, on the other hand, relied on the new relationship with the Allies (since his was the recognized government of China) in an attempt to improve his position against Yen-an. From the end of 1941 until the early months of 1944 he massed his forces to blockade the Red base in the north-west. These years, therefore, were marked by the steady worsening of Kuo-mintang-Communist relations.

In 1944 a Japanese attempt to penetrate the south-west provinces caused Chiang's policy of blockade to be called into question, and led to serious differences between him and the American commander General Joseph Stilwell. Chiang was now compelled to seek a political settlement with the Communists. As the Kuomintang-Communist talks proceeded, the positions of the negotiators grew rigid and further apart. Chiang would not relinquish power, while Chou En-lai, the Communist representative, in-sisted on coalition. The American envoys tried by every means to mediate, but the Kuomintang-Communist cleav-age was too far advanced for their efforts to succeed. When the Japanese surrender came in August 1945, China was hopelessly divided. The glory of victory was overshadowed by the grim struggle between the Kuomintang and the Communists for the control of Occupied China.

The year 1946 was spent in a desperate but futile attempt to save the situation. General George C. Marshall, Ameri-can special envoy, convened a conference in January, and obtained a truce plus promises for a political and military settlement. Hopes were raised that peace might come to China through the broadening of Chiang's government and the integration of the armies. But these hopes were soon dashed. As a result of certain advantages obtained at the Yalta Conference, Soviet Russia gave valuable help to the Chinese Communists as they entered Manchuria. Unwilling to let it go by default, Chiang decided to fight for Manchuria at all costs. Under these circumstances, the January agreements were completely vitiated. As the year drew to an end, hostilities broke out in full force. Marshall declared his mission a failure.

The civil war of 1947-49 was the grand finale, bringing victory to the Communists. Chiang's armies had magnificent equipment and training. But they were no match for the Communist forces, who were supported by the people wherever they went. In Chiang's territory there were runaway inflation and economic dislocation; in Mao's territory there were reform and recovery. This war was truly a débâcle for the Kuomintang. It swept through the eastern third of the country in a series of sanguinary battles, from Changchun and Mukden in Manchuria to Hsuchow and Nanking in the lower Yangtze region. In each of these battles huge Kuomintang armies defected to the Communists, either after they were outflanked or after their supplies were cut by enemy forces in control of the countryside. Reminiscent of the fall of traditional dynasties, military collapse was compounded by the up-surge of economic and social forces repudiating a defunct régime. Early in 1949 Chiang moved the Kuomintang government to Formosa. Nanking fell in April, following which the Communists quickly brought the country under their control. On October 1 the People's Republic was inaugurated in Peking.

Thus the dissolution of the old order had run its course. In broad perspective, the population increase and Western imperialism first undermined the traditional society. Then the Kuomintang sought to reunify the nation along the old grooves without economic and social reforms, only to find itself in a greater predicament than that faced by the Manchu dynasty or by the early Republic. So at the end of a long and arduous journey the initiative for national rejuvenation was seized by the Communists. From 1949 onwards a new age dawned for China, an age of 'socialist transformation' and 'socialist construction'. With this we may leave the past and turn to the present.

3

NEW POWER UNDER COMMUNISM

IN ALL PROBABILITY the nineteen-fifties will go down in history as the most memorable decade in the life of the Chinese nation. As the victorious régime moved from revolution to reconstruction it gave China a powerful re-birth, lifting her people from chaos under the old order to the threshold of modern world power. Indeed, the tumultuous changes made China a Communist nation. But the true purpose was to revitalize an ancient civilization so that China could once again be her own master and become the leading power in Asia. Thanks to the resourcefulness of the leaders, the foundations of new power were laid with remarkable success. In the meantime, however, progress followed a fluctuating curve, showing that China's rise to power, like the rise of other nations to power, had been accompanied by difficulties.

Of all the accomplishments, the first and foremost was the creation of a strong central government with authority directly reaching the people. We may recall that under the old order the landlord-scholar-officials dominated the government, which did little for the welfare of the masses and exercised little control over them. Below the county level the government was actually in the hands of the village elders or the gentry, the family patriarchs, and the officers of the trade or craft guilds. The nation was like a heap of loose sand, unable to cohere as a whole. The contribution of the Communist régime was to put an end to this diffusion of authority, and to tie the top and bottom together by effective means of command and participation.

It took Peking four years to accomplish this task. During 1949-53, while temporarily maintaining a united front with other groups (under the Chinese People's Political Consultative Conference, in accordance with an interim constitution known as the 'Common Programme'), Peking moved with vigour to introduce strong centralized control. The Chinese Communist Party expanded its membership from three million in 1949 to over five million by the end of 1953, and recruited many city workers to transform itself from a vanguard of peasants into a ruling party over the entire people. Having put the Party in a commanding position, a host of mass organizations, viz., the Federation of Trade Unions, the Federation of Cooperatives, the Federation of Democratic Women, the Students' Federation, the Federation of Democratic Youth, and the Federation of Literary and Art Circles, were launched to transmit its orders to the people. Meantime, party workers fanned out into the country to reform the local government. Old village councils, guilds, clan associations, and secret societies were liquidated, and new village governments set up to operate in accordance with directives from Peking.

Accordingly, in 1954 the régime ended the united front and introduced a monolithic state. Nation-wide elections led to the convocation of the National People's Congress, which in turn adopted a Constitution that superseded the 'Common Programme' and is the supreme law of the land today. The government as now constituted rests on the twin hierarchies of the People's Congresses and of the People's Councils. The People's Congresses are elected by the people—by direct vote at the village level, and by indirect vote from the county level up through the provincial level to the highest legislative organ, the National People's Congress. This method of representation is mainly a stage-managed exercise in mass participation rather than popular control of government, because candidates are nominated under the supervision of the Party, and no more than one list of candidates is voted upon. On the other hand, the People's Councils, chosen by the People's Congresses to be the executive branches of government at their respective levels, represent in reality the downward movement of authority from Peking, because they take orders from the State Council at the apex of the hierarchy.

The real driving force behind this government, however, is the tightly knit group of leaders at the top of the Communist Party. These are the men who constitute the Standing Committee of the Politburo of the Party. Especially notable are: Mao Tse-tung, Chairman of the Party; Chou En-lai, Premier; Liu Shao-ch'i, Party theoretician (and since 1959 Head of State); Chu Teh, former Commander-in-Chief of the Red Army; Ch'en Yün, economic overlord; and Teng Hsiao-ping, General Secretary of the Party. These men make policy decisions which are binding on all levels of government and party workers. Their greatest assets are capacity for hard work, thorough understanding of China's problems, dedication to the socialist programme, and ability to reach collective judgement through consultation.

A word must be said about Mao and Chou in particular, because they are the two chief architects of the new China. In Chapter 2 we noted Mao's revolutionary career. In the nineteen-fifties Mao moved from rebel to ruler, making contributions such as he alone could have achieved. He used his prestige to inspire harmony between the military and civilian leaders. He strengthened an expanding Party by weeding out bourgeois elements and fortifying it with a Spartan code of Communist ethics. He turned his followers to new fields of endeavour, and above all, found new techniques for organizing the masses. Thus despite his age (approaching seventy) and frail health,

Mao has remained the rallying centre of direction and inspiration.

Chou En-lai differs greatly from Mao in character and temperament. Descended from a gentry family, Chou is suave, intellectually shrewd but lithe, and by nature absorbed in power strategy. These qualities make him an ideal complement to Mao: the two make a perfect team, one laying the plans, the other pushing them to fruition. One may say that Chou has more than earned his Premiership. He was a prominent student agitator in 1919; helped found the Chinese Communist group in Paris in 1920-22; organized a league of Communist cadets in Canton under the very eyes of Chiang Kai-shek in 1924-26; engineered a series of uprisings in Shanghai, Nanchang, Swatow, and Canton in 1927; and plotted underground activities against Chiang during 1928-31. Every major Communist outbreak bore the imprint of Chou's master mind; the amazing thing was that he invariably survived imprisonment and the sentence of death. In the tangled period of Mao's clashes with the 'Moscow factions' in the Party, Chou moved from one group to another, but always came out on the winning side. From 1931 onwards he settled down as Mao's right hand man. Thenceforth he began two decades of solid work alongside Mao, carrying the burden of the chief administrator and negotiator, first in Kiangsi, then in Yen-an, then in Chungking. Married to Teng Ying-ch'ao, a veteran revolutionary in her own right, Chou's role increased in importance in the years immediately preceding the Communist takeover. In his talks with the Kuomintang and with General Marshall, he pressed Communist demands with such skill that his manœuvres over the conference table literally hastened the Nationalist débâcle on the battlefield.

These are the men at the helm in Peking, who have given real life to the new government. It is leadership of the *élite* in the truest sense of the term. Policies are made in the inner councils of these men rather than in the National People's Congress. Once a decision is made by these leaders, everyone is expected to endorse it and to carry it out. Debate is permitted as to how best to implement the decision, not as to whether the decision is right. The government in China today is therefore not democratic, but authoritarian. Yet we must remember that the greatest yearning of the people has always been for peace and stability, for which they have subordinated the individual self to authority from the centre. This is precisely what is happening today. Despite the concentration of power in the *élite*, the new government makes it possible for China to strive for the maximum development of her strength and to employ that strength for creative purposes. Unity and order can be maintained; productive work can proceed without stop; waste can be eliminated; and the nation's resources can be developed. In short, all avenues for national endeavour are now open.

After the establishment of strong central control, 'socialist transformation' was carried out during the years 1953-57. This was truly a change of overwhelming importance. Replacing private ownership with socialist ownership of all means of production, it not only uprooted the old groups of privilege, but led to a wholesale reorganization of Chinese economy and society. The process of socialization was most spectacular in the field of agriculture. In the few years preceding 1953 the government completed the land reform movement, whereby the land belonging to landlords and rich farmers was confiscated and redistributed to the landless peasants. Then progressive changes were put into effect to carry the peasant masses from individual to cooperative and finally to collective ownership. First, the short-term type of mutual-aid team was introduced. Under this plan, the peasants practised group farming by pooling their labour for the cropping season. In the second stage, the long-term type of mutual-aid team was substituted, making the team permanent rather than seasonal, and pooling draught animals and equipment as well as labour. In both of these stages individual ownership of the land was maintained; but harvests increased in volume because the work teams ensured that no farm was neglected for want of labour just when it was most needed.

The third stage was the low-grade producers' cooperative. Now the pooling of the land took place. This put an end not only to individual selection of crops, but to the ownership of individual harvests. At the close of every season a certain portion of the crop of the entire cooperative was set aside for taxes and for government purchase and the operating expenses of the cooperative were deducted. The balance was divided among the members on the basis of 60 per cent. for labour contributed, 30 per cent. for land, and 10 per cent. for equipment. This represented cooperative ownership. Its prominent feature was the semi-socialist distribution of income, with the amount of land contributed to the cooperative receiving substantial consideration.

The last vestige of individual ownership was eliminated in the fourth and final stage, that is, under the high-grade producers' cooperative (generally known as a ' collective '). All remuneration was now made on the basis of labour only. The members received their income in wages based on the number of labour-day units which they contributed. Thus ownership ceased to be cooperative but became collective, and no opportunity existed any longer for the wealthy peasant to gain more than the poor peasant. (An area less than five per cent. of the total of the collective was generally set aside on which the members could raise vegetables, poultry, etc. as their own produce.) With this the goal of socialization was reached in agriculture. It is interesting to note that at every stage the government measures met with little peasant resistance. This was chiefly because a very large percentage of China's peasants were landless peasants, who accepted socialization because it protected their interests.

While the socialization of agriculture went on apace, a similar process was applied to industry, commerce, and handicrafts. At the end of 1952 the situation in these sectors may be summed up thus: in industry, all the heavy industries and 50 per cent. of the light industries were already under state ownership; in commerce, the state trading companies dominated the wholesale grain and textile markets, but retail trade was privately owned and operated; and in handicrafts, virtually all were in private hands. Therefore during the years 1953-57 the drive for socialization was aimed at the 50 per cent. of light industries still under private ownership, and all of the retail trade and handicrafts. The purpose here was to expand government control of private enterprises until they were taken over by the state.

This process went through two major stages. In the first stage the government placed processing and manufacturing contracts with private industries. The price, quantity, quality, and delivery date of the products ordered were specified in the contracts, while the allocation of raw materials and credits was controlled by the government. In commerce, the government required private firms to serve as sales and buying agencies of the state companies, with price and quality likewise fixed by the government. In handicrafts, cooperatives were formed to facilitate state control in a fashion similar to that pursued in the agricultural cooperatives. Then followed the stage of winning pre-eminent control by the state. This was accomplished by levying increased taxes on all private enterprises. In order to operate, these groups were compelled to seek huge loans from the government; and as a result of this indebtedness, the enterprises lost the major share of their ownership to the state. When the latter took over the planning, management, and production of the enterprises, the task of ' socialist transformation ' was completed. (The former owners of the enterprises were compensated for a certain number of years afterwards with a small percentage of the profits.)

This process of socialization, carried out with remarkable success and within a remarkably short time, immediately put the government in an advantageous position to marshall the productive power of the nation. In one direction, it made central planning feasible because the nation's resources were now at the command of the government. In another, it contributed to greater output. To the latter point Mao Tse-tung attached special importance. The socialization of agriculture and industry could not in itself increase output. But it improved production because no farm was neglected for a single day under the care of group labour, and no factory was allowed to remain idle or to operate with any waste. Thus ' socialist transformation ' was the first step that lifted China to the portals of new power. Now capital accumulation and industrial expansion were within reach.

The First Five Year Plan, which was carried out during the same years of ' socialist transformation ', was a great success. The Plan aimed to increase production in all sectors of the economy. However, emphasis was placed on the development of heavy industries in order to make China strong, and on domestic capital accumulation in order to safeguard her independence. Consumption was drastically cut down and production stepped up through austerity and hard work. Investments in industries were financed with savings from agriculture, while labour productivity was to run higher than increases in wages. The Plan involved a total outlay of £11,000 million. Out of this, over £6,200 million were investments in basic construction: 56 per cent. for industry; 18·7 per cent. for transport and communications; 8·2 per cent. for agriculture; and 17·1 per cent. for other items.

The fulfilment of the Plan exceeded the hopes of the planners. Food grain output rose from 160 million tons in 1953 to 200 million in 1957. Industrial production registered an average increase of 19·2 per cent. per year. Counting the renovated old plants together with the new plants, over 400 major industrial projects were completed during the five year period. As was originally intended, greater strides were made in heavy than in light industry. The following production figures of 1952 compared with those of 1957 illustrate this clearly: steel output rose from 1·3 million to 5·3 million tons; coal output from 64 million to 124 million tons; electric power generating capacity from 7,260 million to 19,000 million kilowatt-hours; crude oil production from 440,000 to 1,440,000 tons; cement production from 2·9 million to 6·7 million tons; metal-cutting machine tools from 13,700 units to 29,100 units. Cotton yarn production, on the other hand, only increased from 3·6 million bales to 4·6 million bales; and cotton cloth from 112 million bolts to 156 million bolts.

The success of the First Five Year Plan led the Communist authorities to seek an unusually ambitious expansion of production as they moved into 'socialist construction' from 1957 onwards. The targets of increased production under the Second Five Year Plan (1958-62) were first announced in 1956. Then in 1957 and 1958 these targets were twice revised upward, until the planners began to speak in terms of a 'major break-through' before the mid-nineteen-sixties. At that time the authorities indeed had every reason for such high hopes. They had encountered no natural calamities of serious proportions. The enthusiasm of the overwhelming majority of the peasant masses produced an annual agricultural surplus, which strengthened the hands of Peking in negotiating with Moscow for industrial and technical aid. True, they recognized that further growth would require the construction of entirely new projects. But they believed that this could be achieved by a greater utilization of the nation's manpower and by cutting down the capital needed for each unit of production. This was the philosophy that inspired the 'Great Leap Forward' campaign in 1958, and the Commune movement which was a part of the same campaign.

The execution of the Second Five Year Plan therefore followed unconventional lines. What was the outcome? For the duration of 1958 and through the autumn of 1959 the 'Great Leap Forward' worked out as the authorities expected. The peasant masses, enthusiastic over the measures of socialization that had defeated the rich and middle peasants, not only supported the new drive with greater incentive, but followed government instructions in adopting new farm implements (such as the deep plough, the united spade, disc harrow, and the three-pronged hoe) and improved methods (such as better seeding, double cropping, and close planting). For the 1958 season food grain production increased from the 200 million tons of the preceding year to 250 million tons. The masses also responded to government directives to set up small-scale, inexpensive industries in the countryside. As a result of smelting done in village furnaces, national production of pig iron increased by 131 per cent. over 1957 and that of steel by 107 per cent. The quality of the local products was inferior, but the overall increase in industrial output was reported to be 60 per cent. Thus in its initial phase the 'Great Leap Forward' contributed much to justify the hopes of the planners in Peking. This may be regarded as the highest point in the upward swing of the development plans in the first decade of the Communist régime.

Beginning with the autumn of 1959, however, an erratic curve began to replace the upward swing. The break seemed to have started in the Communes, but became aggravated by two successive years of drought and flood. The Commune, embracing on the average 5,000 peasant households, was a merger of the collectives within a township (a *hsiang* in Chinese), with emphasis on the total mobilization of its manpower not only for agriculture, but also for industrial operations and military training. Workers were moved about in great numbers and assigned to such gigantic undertakings as building dams and canals, as well as expanded farm work. Under such massive integration of labour the authorities enforced a uniform food ration and minimum wage, and introduced new communal facilities, such as joint kitchens and child-care centres, in order to move large numbers of women to work on the farms or in the village factories. Clearly this ambitious drive was intended further to step up agricultural production, to achieve a tighter control of the life of the people, and to give the rural areas a measure of self-sufficiency in their defence and consumer-goods requirements.

Time may well prove that these objectives were not unattainable under conditions in China. However, in 1959 and the years immediately afterwards a number of factors prevented the changes from operating successfully. The high pressure campaigns which drove the people to do too many things at once caused confusion. Long hours of work, coupled with disruption of family life, led to a lowering of morale and in some instances to physical exhaustion. Further, with tens of thousands of labourers working *en masse*, it became difficult to ensure pride in personal accomplishment. Over-zealousness in administering the strict food ration led to complaints of malnutrition. Still, had it not been for successive years of bad crops it is doubtful whether these factors would have greatly retarded the development of the Communes.

The erratic curve turned into a slump when severe drought and flood hit the nation for two successive years from mid-1959 to mid-1961. Crop damage or loss occurred in half of the agricultural regions throughout the country. Food grain production in 1959 totalled 270 million tons, only a fraction over the 250 million tons of 1958; while in 1960 and again in 1961 it fell below 200 million tons. Thus as a result of administrative over-zealousness, coupled with natural calamities, set-backs occurred in all sectors of the economy. The fulfilment of the Second Five Year Plan was nowhere as successful as that of the First Plan. Since 1961 Peking has not published production figures. During that same year upwards of six million tons of wheat and barley were purchased on the world market to relieve food shortages. Negotiations for Soviet industrial equipment ran into snags due to the weakened position of China's capital accumulation. In April 1962 Chou En-lai told the National People's Congress that the worst crisis was over. But he added that the nation needed to further tighten its belt, to shift more attention from industry to agriculture, to send more people from the cities to work on the farms, and in general to pursue a policy of retrenchment and consolidation. From these facts observers infer that the end result of the Second Plan when published will not fulfil the revised targets of 1958, but will surpass the original targets announced in 1956.

What conclusions are we to draw from this cycle of developments—from the upward swing through an erratic curve then through a slump to retrenchment and consolidation? Clearly it demonstrates the difficulty of sustaining the high rate of growth of the First Five Year Plan. The amazing performance under the latter was to a considerable extent attributable to the speedy recovery from the civil war, the ease of bringing idle pre-war factories back to production, and the newly heightened incentives of the peasant masses following socialization. By the autumn of 1959 these factors had spent their force. Further expansion of the base of production required construction of new factories, yet the capacity for capital accumulation decreased as the haste in the administration of the Communes interfered with the life of the peasant masses. Naturally it became unsound to project further growth on the belief that the upward swing would continue.

Furthermore, during both the First and Second Five Year Plans Peking made little investment in agriculture, but counted upon it to yield huge savings to finance industry. Indeed results were favourable under the First Plan. But the continued exploitation of the agricultural sector gave rise to difficulties under the Second Plan, especially when drought and flood hit the nation. At last the government learned that there is a limit to the extent to which human labour can be utilized to compensate for the shortage of capital. It also realized that the danger of natural calamities is ever-present; whenever they strike they can defeat the most ingenious plans made by men.

It was to the credit of the Communist planners that under the impact of these lessons they immediately adopted more realistic policies. Corrective measures were introduced in the Communes. While administration remained Commune-wide, agricultural production reverted to the smaller but more efficient units of the collectives; 'labour brigades' of 300-400 households were given ownership of their means of production and were no longer continually shifted from one area to another.

Peasants' wages were paid in larger amounts of cash, instead of in food coupons with little cash. Incentive pay and private plots for spare-time cultivation were granted to stimulate production. A rigorous programme was instituted to re-train Party workers in charge of Commune affairs. Meantime, shifting more emphasis from industry to agriculture, the government pushed ahead with vigour such gigantic programmes for flood prevention and for irrigation as the Yellow River project, which when completed will greatly curtail the destructive force of droughts and floods in the agricultural regions of north China. In an effort to conserve soil an ambitious afforestation plan was introduced, to prevent the run-off of rainfall over a million acres of usable land. Similarly to bring more land under cultivation tractors were introduced to plough-up the semi-arid lands in Inner Mongolia and Sinkiang. In short, the régime turned away from sanguine hopes to grapple with concrete realities.

The policy-makers in Peking thus showed a large measure of flexibility and realism. Thanks to retrenchment and consolidation they were able to preserve the gains made in the earlier years. The latest available reports from Peking (1960-1) showed the production of steel at 18 million tons; of coal 400 million tons; of oil 4 million tons; and of electric power 42,000 million kilowatt-hours. As China proceeds with the Third Five Year Plan two broad trends become clear. On the one hand, the leaders in Peking hold firmly to their belief that China's agricultural output can keep up with the increase in her population. Peking's position on the problem of feeding China's population is in direct opposition to that held by Western economists. The Communist authorities argue that despite the limited cultivable land, the per-unit yield will be further increased along with the increase in population. They cite the fact that, excepting the years of natural calamities, food grain production has increased at the rate of 7 per cent. per annum, while the population has increased at the rate of 2¼ per cent. The Communist position is based on the reasoning that under socialism the increase in population will inevitably lead to increase in production, because of the expansion of the labour force and discovery of better methods of production. If this is more than doctrinaire language and proves feasible, then nothing can prevent China from continuing to gain in power and expand her influence in world affairs.

On the other hand, Peking grudgingly accepts a slower pace of industrial growth as inevitable. Peking faces the dilemma of depending on agriculture to finance industry, yet being unable to push agricultural growth to meet such high expectations. The living standards of the people are already very low. Further tightening of the belt to yield an agricultural surplus with which to finance gigantic industrial construction can only be a sluggish process. This is likely to produce recurrent bottlenecks in the execution of future development plans. The validity of these considerations has not been refuted by Peking.

Of course, China has gone a long way towards becoming an industrial power. Foreign ownership and foreign control have become a thing of the past. Pre-war production figures have been left far behind. Factories and mines have spread from coastal cities to the interior in a more rational distribution of industrial sites. But she has yet to throw off the weight of centuries of economic backwardness. China is trying to accomplish in twenty years what it took Britain two hundred years to achieve. Accordingly, she is paying a big price in human sacrifice for the forced development of industries. Not only is she handicapped by marked individual poverty, but shortage of consumer goods has necessitated rationing and tight controls, and has further depressed the standards of living. Neither can she train technicians, engineers, and managerial personnel fast enough to meet the expanding needs. All these facts underscore the position that China is still an underdeveloped country, and as such faces immense hardships in her struggle to build industrial strength within a short time.

A concrete illustration of this aspect is the system of transportation. Her railways and motor highways are far behind the requirements of a modern industrial power. There are less than 3 miles of railway per 100,000 people in China, as compared with 50 miles in European countries, 100 miles in the United Kingdom, and 250 miles in the United States. This compels China to depend on river boats or human and animal carriers, where the cost is inevitably high and the capacity low. A number of trunk rail lines and a large number of highways have been built, notably through Sinkiang, Inner Mongolia, and the northwest industrial regions. But many more are needed. The country is vast, and the cost of construction high. The investments in transportation will continue to be a drain on the nation's capital in the years ahead.

However, in spite of the difficulties confronting China her base for growth is strong. In this connection a definite asset is the abundance of natural resources. China is not as rich in resources as the United States or Soviet Russia. But she has a sufficiently diversified mineral base to become a first-rate industrial power. This encouraging prospect is confirmed by geological findings in the past decade. China has extensive deposits of high-grade coal, estimated at 1,200 billion tons. Her deposits of iron ore have recently been placed at 11 billion tons, and they are located close to coking coal. Oil reserves aggregate 100 million tons, as a result of recent prospecting, but they are situated far away in the interior with no access to railways at the present time. The same is true of hydro-electric power:

potentially important sites are many, but they are located in inaccessible areas and far removed from centres of population. In metals, China has moderate reserves of copper, lead, zinc, and silver. She obtains her sulphur from pyrites. On the other hand, she does have large supplies of manganese, tungsten, tin, antimony, magnesite, and bauxite. As we have said earlier, China definitely possesses the necessary resources to become a first-rate industrial power. The question is: How fast and how far will these resources be developed?

In the field of foreign trade, too, China shows signs of strength and confidence. Prior to 1949 her trade was carried on largely with the Western nations, her imports comprising consumer goods, luxury items, and foodstuffs. Today 75 per cent. of China's foreign trade is carried on with Russia and the countries in the Soviet bloc, over 15 per cent. with Afro-Asian nations, and less than 10 per cent. with countries of western Europe. Her imports now consist mainly of industrial equipment, steel and petroleum products, and rubber. Her exports are made up of hog bristles, eggs, tea, silk, tung oil, and such minerals as tungsten, molybdenum, tin, antimony, and mercury. In years of good harvests China also exports food grains and meat products to Soviet bloc countries, and acts to liquidate her loan obligations by exporting more to Russia than she imports. To Asian countries China has been exporting increasing quantities of light machinery, machine tools, and a variety of consumer goods. As for the pattern of trade, Peking leans heavily to barter. This saves foreign exchange, limits imports, and forces the trading partner to buy from China as well as to sell to her. Thus China is no longer a semi-colonial vassal, but has seized the initiative in her trade relationship with the rest of the world.

Now let us turn to another area of power of the new régime, namely, the evolution of a vigorous foreign policy.

Here China's achievements during the decade under consideration were no less impressive than those in the realm
of internal strength. As under the early Han or early
T'ang, aggressive diplomats in the nineteen-fifties demonstrated what China could do once she acquired unity and
power. At the time of the Communist take-over China had
barely thrown off the last vestiges of imperialist control.
Ten years later she was the strongest power in Asia. That
a diplomatic revolution of such proportions could have
taken place in so short a time can be understood only in
the light of the unique tactical moves of Peking's policy-
makers.

Immediately after the Communist régime was inaugurated it concluded a Treaty of Friendship, Alliance, and
Mutual Assistance with Soviet Russia (February 1950).
This important step was, of course, inspired by ideological
bonds and common interests. Yet its true purpose was to
safeguard China's security. At that time China's diplomacy had only two fronts: *vis-à-vis* Soviet Russia, who
retained a strong influence in Manchuria; and *vis-à-vis* the
United States, who supported the Kuomintang in Formosa. In view of the proximity of Russia, Peking considered it impolitic to alienate this formidable neighbour.
To join with Russia would at least ensure peace along the
Sino-Soviet border, and at best might bring Soviet help in
retaking Formosa. Thus the decision was made to ' lean to
one side ', that is, to align China with Russia and to abandon her traditional friendship with the United States. Of
course, it was recognized that dealing with Russia, especially under Stalin, would not be easy. But to begin with,
close relations were considered a necessity. It was expected
that subsequent years would yield opportunities for seeking a greater independence from the Kremlin.

The alliance thus established soon adopted a policy of
aggression against South Korea and Formosa. At the start

China was interested in Formosa and not directly interested in Korea. But as soon as the attack on South Korea began in June 1950, the United States, answering a United Nations request, despatched troops to Korea to resist the aggression; while American 'neutralization' of the Formosa Strait dashed Peking's hope of taking Formosa. This changed the direction of China's action. She sent her men into Korea to prevent an American victory. Long months of fighting, followed by protracted negotiations, finally ended in the armistice of July 1953, which divided Korea into the Communist north and the anti-Communist south near the 38th parallel.

During this period Chinese diplomacy continued to operate on the same two fronts described above. But surprising developments occurred on each of them. Against the United States Peking nurtured a bitter hatred for its 'interference' in Formosa. Washington on its part pursued a policy of non-recognition and of blocking Peking's entry into the United Nations. In her relations with Soviet Russia, however, China's part in the Korean war unexpectedly gave her a new source of strength. To the chagrin of Stalin, Russia had to permit substantial Chinese influence to enter Korea and Manchuria.

In fact, China's role in the Korean war helped to open a third front in her diplomacy—gaining influence over countries on her borders. Korea, however, was not the only country in this category. Peking had been sending aid to the Communist forces in North Vietnam, who were engaged in a struggle with the French. The latter had been losing one campaign after another since 1946. Finally, in the spring of 1954 France admitted defeat at a conference in Geneva, by recognizing the Democratic Republic of Vietnam. Thus China's pre-eminent influence in North Vietnam became established. In a very real sense this repeated the history of Han and T'ang times, when

Chinese control was effectively maintained over this area.

But no amount of influence in Korea or in Vietnam could make the Communist authorities overlook the situation in Formosa. In 1954-55 this was the prime objective of Peking's diplomacy. The easiest way to invoke help, of course, was to turn to her ally, Soviet Russia. Unfortunately China did not have sufficient influence to demand that Russia implement the alliance obligations. Accordingly Peking searched for new diplomatic ammunition on a fourth front, by arousing the sympathy and support of the Asian nations and utilizing them to weaken the position of the United States. The 'Five Principles of Co-existence' (mutual respect for territorial integrity and sovereignty; non-aggression; non-interference in internal affairs; equality and mutual benefit; and peaceful co-existence) were endorsed in treaties with India, Burma, Indonesia, and others. Premier Chou En-lai made numerous visits to the various countries to cultivate their goodwill. The upshot of this was a war of nerves to force the United States to yield ground on the issues of Formosa and of United Nations membership. The strategy of tension, played by Peking almost to the breaking point, succeeded in keeping most of the Asian nations from joining SEATO (South-East Asia Treaty Organization). But as far as forcing the hand of the United States was concerned, it failed to bring results.

Peking would have tried further to build an Asian bloc against the United States, except that at the Bandung Conference of Afro-Asian nations in 1955 many voices were raised against the 'new colonialism' of Communist China and Russia. The emerging nations strongly objected to power blocs. More specifically, they began to have doubts about China's aggressive moves. They pointed to her invasion of Tibet since 1950, objecting to the imposition of Communist rule, the suppression of the hereditary rights of the Lamaist kingdom, and the confiscation of the properties of the Tibetan people and monasteries. Chou En-lai, being a realist, quickly saw that China would be left in isolation unless she took a ' softer ' approach towards the United States. Accordingly after Bandung a series of talks between the Chinese and American ambassadors began in Geneva (later continued in Warsaw). This phase of Chinese diplomacy was marked by a desire to play for time. To the Asian nations Chou declared that he wished ' to seek common ground and not to create divergence '. Towards the United States, however, this was a change of tactics, not of objective. The Communist representative kept the door shut against any suggestion to recognize ' two Chinas ' (Communist China on the mainland, and Nationalist China in Formosa).

On the eve of the Bandung Conference, however, China's relations with Soviet Russia began to take on a new look. During the life-time of Stalin Russia was reluctant to carry out her promises to aid China. Stalin also kept his hold on Manchuria by supporting certain Chinese leaders opposed to Mao Tse-tung. But China's ability to develop her own strength, as demonstrated both in the Korean war and in China's economic recovery, put an end to this state of affairs. After Stalin's death in 1953 Khrushchev was convinced that a change in Russia's China policy was in order. So during the next five years several visits were paid to Peking by Khrushchev, Mikoyan, and other Soviet dignitaries, to cement closer relations and to offer more generous help. Thus on this front things turned in China's favour. Besides the 50 industrial projects originally pledged by Stalin, the following commitments were added: 91 projects in 1953; 15 in 1954; 55 in 1956; 47 in 1958; and 31 in 1959. (The Russians were to furnish the necessary equipment and technical assistance for their construction; but the Chinese were to pay for them.) The loans and credits extended by Russia to China were limited (totalling about £718 million), but Russia restored to China all her special privileges, such as Manchurian railway rights, the naval base of Port Arthur, and interests in joint-stock companies. On top of these, Russia undertook to build two trunk railways across Inner Mongolia and Sinkiang.

An even greater opportunity for asserting independence from the Kremlin came during the Polish and Hungarian crises in 1956. Chinese officials had long kept watch over Polish affairs, so that when the Posnan revolt broke out Peking's reaction was critical of Russia, accusing her of 'big-power chauvinism'. Later, when the more threatening revolt erupted in Hungary, the Kremlin needed Chinese help. Under the circumstances, China moved from the role of critic to the role of mediator. She still championed 'national communism' and deprecated 'big-power chauvinism'; but she censured Hungary and strengthened the hands of the Kremlin by calling upon all members of the Communist bloc to uphold the sanctity of the Warsaw Pact. What did this add up to in so far as China's diplomatic manœuvres were concerned? The ingenious operations of Chou En-lai substantially elevated China's status and placed her on an equal footing with Russia as the joint arbiters of the Communist world.

Now China felt that her position in relation to Russia had perhaps become sufficiently strong to demand a better performance by Russia as China's ally. In the summer of 1958 renewed tension arose over the off-shore islands in the Formosa Strait. While Khrushchev visited the United States and made preparations for a summit conference, the United States sent missiles and rockets to Formosa, and General Chiang Kai-shek stepped up his forces on Quemoy and Matsu. Peking demanded that Russia do her part as China's ally by helping her with comparable weapons. This put Khrushchev in an embarrassing position. In the end the Soviet leader chose not to supply Peking with new weapons, but warned the United States against arming the Nationalist forces. The Khrushchev letters to President Eisenhower in September 1958 led to the declaration by Secretary of State Dulles that the United States favoured a reduction of Nationalist forces on the offshore islands, and that she would not support any Nationalist plan for the military reconquest of the mainland. This may be considered a qualified victory for Peking. Russia was compelled to honour her treaty obligations, but she fulfilled her duty as China's ally by bringing political, not military, pressure to bear on the United States.

On balance, then, the first decade of China's foreign policy brought accomplishments of far-reaching importance. She succeeded in asserting her independence towards Russia. She maintained with firmness her claim to Formosa. Her close neighbours submitted to her influence, while the outer ring of the Asian nations were ever apprehensive of her power. To be sure, many problems remained to be solved. Russia was wary in meeting China's demands. The United States and the United Nations were unbending in refusing her recognition and admission to the world body. The Asian nations, too, were disquieted over her ambitions. But the basic trend has become indisputable. By dint of her growing strength China has ended the futility of the past and emerged as a new colossus in Asia. Napoleon's dictum that China is a sleeping giant who once awakened will shake the world begins to merit some thought.

4

THE FUTURE IN THE MAKING

WITHOUT DOUBT THE resurgence of China will be a long continuing process, of which the progress made in the nineteen-fifties marked but the beginning. Yet a sufficiently firm foundation has been laid to exert an enduring influence on future developments. In a real sense, the nineteen-fifties gave China a breathing spell, because no outside forces—neither Japan nor the Western powers nor the emerging nations of Asia—were in a position to interfere with her endeavours. This golden opportunity was seized and utilized to full advantage by a strong government with a strong programme. Having caught the psychological moment at the right juncture, China turned away once for all from defeat to victory, from a century of chaos to a fresh era of achievement.

No less important than the time factor is the nature of the changes that occurred in this crucial decade. When the Second World War ended nationalism held sway over half of Asia, bringing about revolutions in many countries. But in many cases, as for instance, Indonesia and Burma, the nationalist movements stopped short after the overthrow of imperialism. Political instability and economic dislocation retarded the work of nation-building. China, on the other hand, successfully developed a national unity and a creative purpose. Her homogeneity of sentiment transformed itself into a homogeneity of objective and accomplishment. Thus China, unlike other nations, did make the significant advance from the destructive to the constructive stage of nationalism.

Further, the strength of the new régime is deeply rooted.

If we compare it with the Bolshevik régime in Russia, we see this clearly. The Bolsheviks seized power in 1917 in what was in essence a conspiracy, and had to spend a decade defending the revolution. The Chinese Communists, however, took power after they had fought and won a long drawn-out revolution. As a result the Peking government based itself upon a reserve of genuine strength from the start. Again, if we compare this régime with modern Japan, we can draw another instructive lesson. Japan owed the greater part of her industrial growth to the First World War, whereas China's progress rested not on chance but on her own hard work. As we have seen, Soviet aid came to her after, not before she proved her ability to accumulate her own capital. For these reasons, no rival group has effectively challenged the régime.

There is little evidence to support the view that the new régime will collapse or wither away in short order. To be sure, expressions of discontent are by no means lacking. In 1956-57, for example, when the government eased restrictions on freedom of speech, many intellectual leaders spoke out against Peking's dictatorial policies and close ties with Moscow. The régime has also pushed a campaign to 'brainwash' those who cling to traditional or Western cultures. Yet as the years go by the forces of opposition have failed to rally or triumph over the forces of control from above.

Perhaps the main reason is to be found in the sustained vitality of the Communist leadership. In 1954-5, for example, the Party emerged with a greater unity after removing Kao Kang and other dissident elements in Manchuria. Two years later the solidarity of the Party leaders was further demonstrated at the Eighth Party Congress. Since then, in every drive that brought difficult problems,

---

7. *Transport, old and new.* The thirty hundredweight lorry is a proto-type about to go into mass production in Shanghai.

7a

7b

8a

8b

the Party members (eighteen million in 1962) have maintained their unity through self-criticism and self-reform. In the government, too, its stability is demonstrated in the peaceful transfer of power: Liu Shao-ch'i succeeded Mao Tse-tung as Chairman of the Republic in 1959 and worked harmoniously with Chou En-lai, who continued his tenure as Premier.

For a number of reasons one may expect this state of affairs to continue for years to come. The immensity of the new tasks ahead creates new challenges and keeps up a high morale among large segments of the population. The endless call for heroism and self-sacrifice facilitates the rule of the present leaders because it sustains a crusading ardour. Meantime, a new tradition of respect by military as well as civilian officials for centralized control contributes immeasurably to strengthen the authority of Peking. Today generals rise and fall without questioning the orders from above. There is no suggestion of insubordination, let alone revolt. This must be considered one of the greatest accomplishments of the Communist government. Similarly, the pre-eminence of the Communist Party over the small political parties is thoroughly established. This is because the small parties in China, unlike the Mensheviks or Social Revolutionaries in Russia, do not possess real power. The Communist authorities actually encourage their existence, while at the same time making use of them to absorb former bourgeois elements into the new socialist state.

In Chapter 3 we have seen that the system of government today represents a negation of democracy. The Communists are practising a Chinese type of authoritarianism

---

8. *Silk weaving, old and new.* It is interesting to compare this hand-loom with the much more primitive one shown in Plate 4, and both of them with the modern power-driven machinery. The machine is unwinding the silk from the cocoons of the silkworms and winding it on to spools ready for weaving.

which, neither granting individual liberty nor going to extremes of tyranny, proved efficacious in past epochs of greatness and power. Peking's leaders believe that, in view of the lack of individual initiative of the masses in China, political democracy or economic *laissez-faire*, however great their intrinsic merits, can only lead to chaos. Like the strong rulers of the past, they hold that the *élite* must lead and determine the objectives of group endeavour. Hence the hue and cry for organization, the drives for production, and the innumerable campaigns for socialist instruction and training.

On the other side of the ledger, the Chinese type of authoritarianism keeps the use of violence to a minimum. Again like the strong rulers of the past, the Communist authorities today consider forcible coercion, such as that used by Stalin in Russia, both ineffective and impermissible under Chinese conditions. In a historic speech in 1957 Mao Tse-tung said that the government of course reserves the right to punish the enemies of the people for reaction, subversion, or any other violation of the principles of socialist construction. But aside from this, he urges persuasion and education as better instruments of government than coercion. In his view it is more effective for the government ' to issue suitable orders of an obligatory nature '. Here is perhaps the best example of how the leaders in Peking are adapting traditional Chinese authoritarianism to meet present-day needs, or to put it differently, how they are twisting and adjusting twentieth-century totalitarianism to fit the Chinese temperament and tradition.

To illustrate the point, political police as an instrument of terror play a relatively insignificant role in China today. The Campaign against Counter-revolutionaries in 1951 was quickly wound up, after serving as a shock treatment to the public. Since then a small percentage of former landlords and capitalists have been put through periods of corrective labour in order to 'punish few and reform many'. Actually, since the entire nation accepts orders for hard work, there is little need for terror. Rather the government empowers the public security bureaux to take the census, maintain registration forms, check the people's movements, mediate disputes, and mobilize the masses for public welfare work. In addition, the government calls innumerable meetings or 'study groups' to 'reason' with the people, to explain the government's policies, and in general to inculcate the socialist way of life. So Communist statecraft avoids overt force while it seeks to supervise the people's lives and win their minds. Today, as in the past, the people are accustomed to discipline and proper group behaviour, and amenable to orders from above. There is reason to believe that the Communist government will continue to rule by converting the people rather than by terrorizing them, by encouraging them to be more obedient rather than destroying them for not being obedient enough.

This should provide an answer to the frequent query: What is the future destiny of Communism in China, and will it be tempered by Chinese tradition? The avoidance of ruthless measures of the Stalinist type appears to be the unquestioned approach. But government control is tight, and since it is maintained by non-violent means, it promises to remain tight for a long time to come. Thus one may conclude that the Communist rule in China, while less harsh and less extreme, is likely to last much longer without a 'thaw' than that in Soviet Russia. Unless there develop fresh abuses of power in Peking or a total economic collapse, neither of which is within sight, the present régime is destined to stay in power with undiminished authority for a long time.

The area which deserves close observation today is the

Commune. It is unfortunate that immediately after the Commune movement began serious droughts and floods hit the nation. This confused the issue and led many prematurely to call the movement a failure. Actually the Communist authorities have not at all abandoned the programme. As we have seen, they have taken steps to introduce corrective measures. Ultimately the Communes may well prove to be the permanent form of socialism in China.

In what direction is the Commune movement likely to produce significant new developments in China? The answer probably lies in the emergence of an unprecedented village economy against a background of the industrialization of a vast under-developed country. The Communist planners have now put agricultural and non-agricultural operations in the Communes on two separate bases. As far as agriculture is concerned, the production unit has reverted to the collective, where smaller labour-brigades lend themselves to more efficient management. However, in the non-agricultural operations (that is, in administration, village industries, public works, and military training), the functioning of the Commune as a unit has been strengthened. Positive advantages are expected from this. By integrating the labour force of the whole township, a Commune can undertake large-scale construction projects without being handicapped by jealousies among the various collectives. Coordination of rural industries and military training is administered to better effect by the Commune than by the collective. In the field of handicrafts, the larger unit of integrated labour and the control of minimum wage-payments in the Commune are conducive to mass production at lower costs. On the basis of his years of experience with peasant masses, Mao Tse-tung maintains that the larger the peasant economic unit, the greater its production of consumer goods. This principle is being vigorously pushed in the Communes today. The outcome may be to reduce inflationary pressure while the government carries out its programme of rapid industrialization.

The significance of the Commune movement, then, seems to lie in subsidiary industrialization in the very midst of agriculture. The long-term effect can be the attainment of self-sufficiency in the tens of thousands of villages, resulting from the merging of farming and consumer-goods production in one and the same locality. In such an event the need for allocating city manufactures to the country will be reduced to a minimum, and with it the tension that normally exists in a society undergoing forced industrialization. When this stage of development is reached, then the Chinese will have advanced farther on the road to communism in accordance with a programme different from that followed by the Soviets. So the Commune movement may conceivably ease some of the difficulties of China's industrialization which we have noted in Chapter 3. It may even enable China to bypass what orthodox Marxists regard as the necessary stages before reaching the goal of combining agriculture with industry and abolishing the distinction between town and country.

In the midst of all this, the relationship between the government and the people is rapidly reaching a new equilibrium. The government imposes hard work on the people and takes a lion's share of their output to pay for national reconstruction. At the same time, it regulates the people's livelihood and provides state-supported services to ensure a measure of social well-being. A citizen must obey the law, pay taxes, serve in the armed forces, and protect state property. Meantime, he is guaranteed the right to work, to rest, to education, and to social security benefits. Thus, while an atmosphere of austerity pervades the nation and while the government rules with a strong hand, the people accept its rule with little opposition. The situation is anything but *laissez-faire*. But it is an improvement upon the old order wherein the ruling class neglected the masses and promoted their own interests. This is why there is no revolt; the bulk of the population does not find the new masters unacceptable.

Today the relationship between the government and the peasant may be explained in simple terms. The government receives from the Communes a tax in kind, computed at a fixed percentage of the 'normal' yield, ranging between 16 per cent. and 25 per cent. depending on the different regions. In addition, the government makes compulsory purchases of the products of the Communes at low government-fixed prices. From time to time the government also demands special contributions or levies. All told, the peasant turns in to the government approximately 45 per cent. of his harvest, which is practically the same amount he used to turn in to his landlord in pre-Communist days. The government then sells the food grains to city consumers at an increased price, and uses the profit for industrial construction.

On the peasant's part, however, his new relationship with the government has brought significant changes in his life. Instead of holding the insecure tenancy on a fragmented plot, he is one of a large labour force working in the Commune under a central plan. Instead of working less than 200 days a year, he now works practically 365 days. As we have seen, he surrenders to the government a portion of his harvest equivalent to what he used to surrender to his landlord. As a result, his living standard has not shown any marked improvement. However, with increased crop yields in the years of normal climatic conditions, his annual grain consumption has risen from 420 lbs. to 600 lbs., even though meat and poultry are luxuries he cannot have. He need no longer be concerned with debts. The government gives a minimum of relief when famine strikes or in the care of the sick, disabled, and aged. The one important condition required by the government is that he must do his share of productive work.

A comparable situation exists in the relationship between the government and the industrial worker. In the old days the work day was often fourteen or sixteen hours long. Now eight hours is the standard, although in the frequent drives for greater production it runs to ten or eleven. A non-skilled worker earns an average of 40 yuan per month, compared with 15 yuan before 1949; and a skilled worker now earns an average of 80 yuan per month, compared with 30 yuan before 1949. (£1 equals 6.85 yuan today.) True, the life of the city worker is by no means a free or easy one. There is the ever-pressing demand for higher production, without wage increases to match. Trade unions are task-masters enforcing government orders rather than independent agents championing the rights of the working men. Most of the leisure time is consumed in meetings for political training. Consumer goods are in short supply and the living standard continues to be low. Nonetheless, the thirty-odd million industrial workers are more secure under the present régime. This is because they are now working under improved physical conditions, with effective measures for accident prevention and for medical care. Insurance programmes have been instituted providing for hospital treatment, sick leave, disability compensation, maternity leave, old-age benefits, and death benefits. The government gives the worker security of employment, and has been constantly improving his housing situation. Most important of all, the worker has developed a sense of pride in the work he performs : he feels himself to be part of the national rejuvenation as he sees the nation grow in power and stature.

Two areas in which the new régime has made important

progress are health and education. In the old days elementary sanitation and public hygiene were grievously neglected, and many people died every year of epidemic diseases. Today, following intensive drives to establish sanitary latrines, to exterminate rodents, flies, and mosquitoes, and to forbid spitting, the incidence of cholera, malaria, dysentery, tuberculosis, and trachoma has been greatly reduced. The cities and villages in China are now cleaner than they have ever been in her long history. As far as curative medicine is concerned, the régime is making steady progress, although the results achieved so far are still inadequate. For example, in spite of the feverish training programme, only 100,000 physicians in Western medicine and 500,000 physicians in traditional herb medicine (who carry on their practice after receiving a certain amount of modern training) are available today. There are only 500,000 hospital beds in the entire country. Thus China has a long way to go in the field of medicine. Nevertheless, the important point is that the unfortunate state of the past is coming to an end.

In the field of education China has long been a country of two extremes. While less than ten per cent. of the population produced her great scholars and teachers, ninety per cent. of the people were illiterate. Through the centuries nothing effective was done to improve the situation. The progress being made today comes under several headings. First, the Communist régime regards the regular system of schools as the training ground for the new intelligentsia. Accordingly, the state spends large sums of money for the support and expansion of these schools. Today there are 100 million pupils in primary schools (4 times the 1949 figure); 14 million in secondary schools (7 times the 1949 figure); and over 3/4 million in colleges and universities (5 times the 1949 figure). Compulsory primary education is the policy in effect today. Besides the regular

schools, there are 'spare-time schools' of all types. Operated at a minimum cost, these schools bring adult education to the farms, factories, offices, and wherever feasible.
At present 75 million are enrolled in these *ad hoc* schools,
under the slogan 'work diligently and conduct schools
frugally'.

Last but not least is the nation-wide campaign against
illiteracy. Lists of simplified ways of writing the Chinese
characters (words) have been periodically issued by the
government to enable more people to learn the written
script. In addition, a basic vocabulary of the most fre-
quently used characters is taught to thousands of illiterate
people in short but intensive courses. Upon completing
the work, the students turn instructor to teach others the
same basic vocabulary. It is hoped that within ten years
every citizen will be able to read the simplest directives
of the government.

This ambitious bid to widen the scope of education has
not been an easy task. There has been a continuous shortage of teachers. In spite of the large funds spent, school
buildings are inadequate. But the authorities speak with
pride of the quality of performance. Certain aspects of
the current educational policies of the Chinese government deserve mention. For one thing, stress is placed on
implanting socialist doctrine in the minds of men. As a
result humanistic studies and the social sciences receive
very different treatment in Chinese schools from that in
schools of the West. On the other hand, the development
of science and technology receives the greatest encourage-
ment. Considering how much China lagged behind the
Western nations in these fields before the Second World
War, even the modest number of scientists (50,000) and
engineers (30,000) which she has today is a sign of progress.
No doubt larger numbers will graduate from the universities in the years ahead to swell their ranks. Attention is

focused on all branches of science and technology, as is shown in the long-term plan of the National Science and Technology Commission, which is the policy-making body directing the development of sciences. Research institutes have multiplied rapidly in recent years. Some of them, engaged in electronics, nuclear physics, geological, and chemical research, have earned international recognition for their work. Although Soviet assistance has had great influence in bringing about these strides, Chinese scientists have been tapping every possible source of learning from other countries.

Recent reports suggest that China may soon explode her own atomic bomb and send her own space ship into orbit. When she achieves these triumphs of technology, she can throw off the age-old stigma of being backward in scientific accomplishments. We may recall that in ancient and mediæval times the Chinese made important inventions, such as the mariner's compass, the art of printing, and gunpowder. It was the obscurantism of the bureaucratic state and Neo-Confucianist philosophy that stifled science while Europe forged ahead in the ages of the Renaissance, the Reformation, and the Industrial Revolution. Now it seems that history has turned full circle. With the demise of the old society and the old ideas, the inventiveness of the Chinese mind is once again proving its ability to compete with the scientists of the world.

Current Chinese education policy also stresses the integration of mental work with manual labour. Students are told that while reading and studying they must not forget production; that theory must not be divorced from practice; and that mental exercise is incomplete without physical exercise. Very often whole classes of students are sent to work in the villages on a mixed study-and-work plan. The sociological significance of this movement can be understood only if we bear in mind the silent revolution going on to bring up the cultural level of the vast country-side. At a time when industrial centres are rising and urbanization gaining momentum, China is taking this step to close the gap between the country and the city by introducing educated leadership into rural areas. Sending college students to work on the farms is prompted not so much by the need to provide additional labour as by the desire to make the villages culturally more advanced and hence more attractive to people from the cities. This will inevitably reduce town-country tension, thereby adding strength to the nation as a whole. Here again the educational policy is conceived in a manner to complement the newly-emerging pattern of the village, as mentioned above in connection with the Communes.

The creation of the new society is intimately bound to the emancipation of women. Under the marriage law of the new régime women enjoy full equality with men in the selection of their mates, in the right to initiate divorce, and in family responsibility, social status, and ownership of personal property. The wife is no longer the inferior partner, with her rights and happiness hanging precariously on the mercy of her husband. What has really caused this social revolution is the new opportunities for work open to women. Today they have emerged from behind the courtyard to take up jobs in offices, in factories, or on the farms. The economic independence of Chinese women is the true cause of their emancipation. Because they have become economically independent, they are socially and legally independent.

This economic causation of social change also explains the emergence of the conjugal family as contrasted with the patriarchal family of old. We hear so often about the destruction of the family by the Communist rulers. This is a sweeping statement. What is happening is the substitution of a new family unit for the old, and the responsible factor is economic. In the old days, prior to socialization, the patriarchal family with several generations under one roof was an integral unit of production and consumption. Since all members of this unit had to stick together for their livelihood, naturally there were clan loyalty, filial piety, and ancestor worship. Today, with the abolition of private means of production and with consumption based upon wages received from the state, the family has shrunk to the conjugal unit of husband, wife, and their children. The state maintains nurseries and schools to take care of the children during the working day; it also maintains homes for the aged to care for the parents. A family's economic ties are now with the state rather than with the clan. As a result the people are drawing away from their elders: filial piety and ancestor worship have receded into the background. The social values of the Chinese today have come to resemble those held by the peoples of other socialist countries in the world.

The Communist authorities, however, do uphold a policy calculated to foster social change in other directions. Most noteworthy is the training of youth. After an initial period when Party zealots encouraged youngsters to repudiate their parents, more constructive programmes have been instituted in recent years to train the youth not only in Communist ideology, but in practical lessons on rendering service to the state. The guiding motto of the 30 million odd members of the Young Pioneer Corps, for instance, is to love their fatherland, their people, the public property, science, and labour. The young people are taught that the individual exists for the country, that learning must enable them to fulfill their responsibilities as the future pillars of the socialist state.

In the fields of art, literature, and religion the régime has taken strong measures to control thought and mould men's minds. Many eminent scholars and thinkers of the

old school or with a Western liberal bent have been subjected to strenuous pressure of state indoctrination. They
have been made to confess their past ' errors ' by repudiating the intellectual traditions of the past and praising the
new socialist dogma. Old history, poetry, and paintings
that fail to bring out the heroism of the impoverished
masses have been downgraded as bourgeois. Meanwhile
frantic efforts are made to encourage creative work by
writers and artists with proletarian backgrounds. New
plays are written on themes dealing with group farming,
competitive drives in factories, and the like. These efforts
to create a new art and a new literature from the masses
and for the masses, however, have not yet shown any true
merit, perhaps because the policy of discouraging art for
art's sake inhibits creativity.

As for religion, there have been no conflicts of major
consequence. As we have seen in Chapter 1, neither Confucianism nor Buddhism nor Taoism is an organized
religion. They have no politically conscious theology to
clash with the ideology of the government. Nor do they
have any entrenched power to offer resistance to socialization. The government has experienced little difficulty in
confiscating the land of the Buddhist monasteries or in
taking over Buddhist temples for use as offices or schools.
The Buddhist monks and Taoist priests have accepted
government orders to abandon their profession, and have
taken up productive jobs along with lay citizens. (In
Peking a Chinese Buddhist Association sponsors Com-
munist-guided activities for Buddhist circles, perhaps to
impress Buddhist countries in South-East Asia.) The
régime indeed allows certain harmless ceremonies and
sacrifices to continue among the older folk, but it knows
well that they do not appeal to the youngsters and will
die out. As for the Christian Churches, however, the Communists accused them of subversion and waged a relent-

less war against them in the nineteen-fifties by expelling most of the foreign missionaries and jailing the rest. To-day Chinese Christians are led by those who will collaborate with Peking.

Up to this point we have discussed changes wrought in the old social order. Now we must turn to areas of new activity and new growth. We have learned earlier that the western two-thirds of the country are non-agricultural, and that traditionally they formed a power vacuum because the government in China Proper never developed a policy to control them owing to its lack of interest in deserts, steppes, and mountains. Today this attitude has been reversed. New industrial centres are being developed in the north-west. Railways and highways are being con-structed across the vast expanse of these regions. Further, diligent prospecting by geologists has found new deposits of oil and other mineral resources in these areas, so that ambitious programmes for their development have been put into operation.

Accordingly, Peking pursues a policy to integrate the non-Han minorities of these regions with the centre of power in China Proper. Although this has been disguised by establishing 'autonomous regions', giving the local population control of their own culture in return for accepting political and economic control by Peking, the change is truly revolutionary in character. Inner Mon-golia was the first to come under tight control. Sinkiang followed next. Tibet was the last to be integrated. Here the building of strategic highways and other preparatory work took time, while the resistance led by the Dalai Lama held out until 1959, when the Tibetans' last proud stand was crushed by the superior forces of the Communists.

Thus alongside the socialist transformation of China Proper, a great movement for the development of the west is going on. From the regional standpoint, we note the rise of an industrial belt in the Shensi-Kansu-Ninghsia-Suiy-uan area (historically the stamping ground of nomad invaders); the development of oil in Sinkiang and Chinghai (until recent years an area of Russian encroachment); the steady influx of engineers and technicians into these pastoral lands; and a rapid step-up in the educational and cultural levels of the Uighurs, Mongols, and Tibetans. From the national standpoint, the cleavage between an agricultural society and a nomadic society is fast giving way to an integrated power complex that sits astride the industrial west and the agricultural east, and commands the strategic advantage of a continuous land mass with interior solidarity. Psychologically, too, the Chinese are turning pioneers. The mass inertia that persisted for many centuries is disappearing. Prepared to face frontier hardships, young men and women are going west—to test their luck in new lands, and to build a promising morrow by taming the wilderness.

The Communist régime must also be credited with revolutionizing China's defence establishment and strength. The army system of pre-Communist days was one of hired mercenaries who preyed on innocent people and had no sense of loyalty to the state. The Communists have radically changed the situation. From the early days of their revolution the Red Army and the guerrilla units operated as true national forces : they were from the people and for the people. Since 1949 this spirit has been further strengthened. A new conscription law replaced voluntary recruitment with universal military service. The sons of non-agricultural families as well as those of peasant origin have entered the ranks of the army. Close to three million men serve in the regular army. The Communist soldier of today is an honoured citizen, well fed and clothed, and socially esteemed. He is ready to defend the country in time of war as well as to help with reconstruction in time of peace. The services they have performed in building roads and water-conservation works, in promoting sanitation and public hygiene, and in teaching improved farming methods illustrate the successful fusion of the military and civilian population, which is a spectacle never witnessed before in Chinese history.

As for the guerrilla forces, they have lost their *raison d'être* upon the unification of the country. On the other hand, militia corps have been set up in every village, county, and city. The members of the militia are men and women who have undergone certain basic military training. Their function in peace time is to help maintain order and security, safeguard production, promote reconstruction, and carry out army enlistment. The militia corps are trained and supported by the people at no cost to the government, but they form a tremendous reservoir of fighting personnel who can be called upon to augment the regular army whenever necessary.

The equipment of the Chinese armed forces presents a somewhat mixed picture. The ground forces possess first-rate fire power, thanks to a well-organized artillery. The air force has been gaining in strength, with more than 2,000 jet planes. However, it is deficient in the latest models of bombers, with their very high speeds. China has only short-range ballistic missiles, supplied by Russia, which also controls the atomic warheads. The Chinese navy is weak, although a beginning has been made in this direction. At present, emphasis is placed on vessels for coastal defence, landing craft, and submarines.

In view of these deficiencies and weaknesses in various respects, what conclusion can we draw? Experts agree that for a number of years to come China will not be able to carry out an offensive war against such major powers as the United States or Soviet Russia. On the other hand, she possesses great strength in ground warfare. This means that she is virtually indestructible when it comes to the defence of her own land, or even in fighting localized wars in countries on her borders. Military observers point to the fact that China's men of military age (90 million strong) are twice the number in Russia or three times the number in the United States.

All this bulging expansion and increase of power have heightened China's international status. In Chapter 3 we have seen how during the first decade of its existence the new régime elevated China's position among the nations. Today, in the second decade, the world wonders where this rising power is heading. In this connection, many perplexing questions are being asked. Will China use force to take Formosa? Will she break with Russia? Will she seek to control her Asian neighbours through subversion or trade? There is even a school of thought which argues that China wishes for a war to destroy both the United States and Russia, in order to make herself the remaining great power. Such queries and conjectures reflect a state of anxiety without probing into the true substance of Chinese foreign policy.

China is seeking both aggressively and realistically to make herself the leading power in Asia. After a decade of hard-earned achievement her desire is to consolidate her gains and to tackle the more deeply-rooted problems which lie ahead. This is why the earlier jingoism is now combined with an inner toughness. It seems that the objective of Peking's foreign policy is to have a period of world peace, but to utilize local or border wars to increase her power in Asia so that she can claim a major share of influence alongside Russia and the United States. We need not be unduly concerned over a world holocaust, but perhaps should look for the struggle for a redistribution of world leadership among three rather than two great powers. The issue is not whether China might provoke a world war—obviously it is beyond her means to bring the United States or Russia to fight one another—but how and to what extent she will be able, or will be permitted, to become the dominant power in Asia.

When we put the matter in this light, many interesting aspects of the problem come into relief. The power realignment envisaged by China involves tremendous stakes. Neither the United States nor Russia is willing to yield ground unless a day is reached when China's strength compels them to do so. Yet during the interval it is impossible for China to modify her objective as long as she is gaining in strength. Thus the prospect is one of protracted confrontation of pressures from different directions. How far, how fast, and in what direction China will be able to satisfy her aspirations depends upon the interplay and relative strength of these pressures.

Perhaps the area of greatest interest is the alliance relationship with Russia. We must not assume that a split is likely to occur. China cannot afford to alienate Russia, nor can Russia afford to lose China as her ally. Yet among the Soviet leaders today there is a genuine fear of China's growing strength. We have seen how since the late nineteen-fifties the Kremlin has set serious limits to her aid to Peking. In the field of weapons, in particular, China is disappointed in her hopes of Soviet assistance. This is the real reason why the relations between the two allies are unsettled. On the surface the Moscow-Peking controversy is ideological. Chinese theoreticians call Khrushchev naïve when he says that war with the capitalist countries is not inevitable. They attack Khrushchev's endorsement of peaceful co-existence as dangerous. When Moscow charges that Peking's 'hard line' is 'dogmatism', Peking counter-charges that Moscow's 'soft line' is 'revisionism'. All these polemical exchanges reflect China's dissatisfaction with the Soviets' lack of diligence in helping her on such issues as her claim to Formosa. A victim of the continued boycott by the United States and the United Nations, China feels that the Soviet line can only serve to perpetuate her weakness in the family of nations.

Thus a struggle is on to determine whether Russia should go all out to help China achieve supremacy in Asia, or whether China should accept a more modest line by reducing her ambitions. If China is able to bring Russia closer to her point of view, then increased Chinese pressure for the reduction of American power in Asia will be the inevitable outcome. If the two retain their different positions, the effect will be for China to strive towards her goal unaided, a circumstance which can only retard her power build-up. In all probability the latter appears to be the pattern of things to come, and the alliance relationship between China and Russia seems destined to simmer in protracted arguments without destroying the basic bonds of association.

If Russia is reluctant to satisfy China's aspirations, even more so is the United States. The deepening cleavage between China and the United States over the years can only be understood in the light of their conflict of interests in Asia. Peking insists upon American withdrawal from Formosa, refuses to consider a 'Two Chinas' settlement, and repeatedly asserts that it will wait any length of time to 'liberate' the island from American domination. Just as tenaciously Washington is committed to the defence of Formosa, supports the Kuomintang government as a member of the United Nations, and retards the process of admitting Communist China into the world body. Peking evidently hopes that one day internal revolt will topple the Kuomintang régime, enabling it to take the island, deliver a blow to American prestige, and make its entry into the United Nations as the victor. But no one can tell when or whether such an eventuality will occur, and the United States doggedly persists in her policy of non-recognition. Even such vital considerations as the need for an effective arms control agreement have not led Washington to reverse its boycott of Peking. Thus the stalemate on this front is rigid indeed, posing an almost insuperable obstacle to the fulfilment of China's aspirations.

Under these circumstances it is no wonder that Peking is now moving in other directions, particularly in South-East Asia, to score victories in order to compensate for her set-backs against the United States and Russia. From the standpoint of power politics this latest trend may lead to important consequences. In the Indo-Chinese peninsula, which is the avowed sphere of operation of SEATO, Chinese power has made serious inroads and shows every sign of continued extension. In Laos the pro-Communist groups, who are backed by China's satellite in North Vietnam, have all but destroyed the power of the Royal Laotians, who are tied to the United States. If we move south-eastward beyond the Laotian battlefront, large numbers of guerrillas have risen against the government of South Vietnam, whose American-trained forces are hard put to stem the revolutionary tide. Cambodia and Burma are struggling to maintain a neutralist stand, although they are increasingly wary of Chinese might. As for Thailand, the proud bastion of SEATO, Communist China is known to have fostered a Pan-Thai movement inside Yunnan, which one day may attempt to seize power in Bangkok. China, then, is playing for big stakes in this area. What she cannot gain in Formosa may well be offset by fresh victories in South-East Asia.

Several important consequences may result from this situation. First, it can pose an increasing threat to the SEATO powers. The 'umbrella' of protection held by SEATO was structurally weak to begin with. When the battle is joined it will be a contest between a power on the spot, with the advantage of short, interior lines of communication, and its opponents with bases far away, depending on long, exterior lines of sea and air support. Seldom in history has a comparable situation ended in favour of the latter.

Second, if China succeeds in winning over these nations that are predominantly Buddhist, she may be emboldened to increase her pressure upon India. Peking, critical of India's acceptance of Western aid and ever ready to attack her borders, has led some observers to stress her eagerness to goad India into heavy defence spending, to retard her economic development, and above all to call a halt to large-scale Soviet aid to India. Viewed in this light, Peking's ultimate objective is to attempt to compel India to accept Chinese leadership in Asia instead of permitting her to become a rival centre of influence.

In another direction China's success in the Indo-Chinese peninsula can have repercussions on her relations with Soviet Russia. Ever since the mid-nineteen-fifties a conflict of policies has raged between Russia and China regarding the direction of Communist movements in the South-East Asian countries. Russia advocates the promotion of communism in these countries not by subversion, but by joining with bourgeois nationalist movements and participating in parliamentary elections. China takes strong exception to this line. Her policy is to take no part in bourgeois elections or nationalist governments, but to continue subversion by working with the revolutionary masses. What is going on today seems to prove China's point. The Communist gains in Laos have been obtained by following Mao's revolutionary pattern. The increasing power of the guerrillas in South Vietnam may also be taken as a vindication of the Mao line. Should China make greater inroads in this area, the Soviets will have to forfeit much of their leadership over China's Asian neighbours.

China, then, is losing no time in her bid to become the leader in Asia. As we have seen, the implementation of her policy runs into serious difficulties with the United States. Soviet Russia guards herself against China's growing strength. With other nations, however, China's relations are marked by little tension. She has no quarrel with Great Britain. London's early recognition of the régime and relaxation of trade restrictions since the mid-nineteen-fifties, coupled with the understanding of the Chinese situation by the British people, have led Peking to regard Britain as a potential friend. Peking is content to leave Hong Kong as a British colony: while London takes pride in holding on to this empire outpost, Peking uses it as a convenient front for trade and contact with the West. With regard to Japan, Peking is irked by her ties with the United States, but believes that eventually Japan can be disengaged from these commitments. China regards Japan as a future source of non-Soviet aid. Moreover, should China win dominion over the Indo Chinese peninsula, that will further narrow Japan's world market, thereby making her more amenable as a trading partner.

Thus China's international position faces both perils and promises. Whether she will break through her difficulties with the United States and Russia may well be determined by the new strength she acquires internally, in South-East Asia, and among other friendly nations. One point, however, seems clear. Her ambition to become the leading power in Asia will continue to add to international tension in the years ahead.

SUGGESTIONS FOR FURTHER READING

FACTUAL

NATHANIEL PEFFER: *China: The Collapse of a Civilization* (Routledge, 1931). Trenchant analysis of the dissolution of the old order.

LIN YUTANG: *My Country and My People* (Heinemann, 1936). Witty and delightful portrayal of life and society in traditional China, applicable largely to the cultivated class rather than to the masses.

LIN MOU-SHENG: *Men and Ideals: An Informal History of Chinese Political Thought* (Day, New York, 1942). A study of the development of Chinese political thought, with pointers to areas of common interest between Chinese and Western thinkers.

KENNETH SCOTT LATOURETTE: *The Chinese: Their History and Culture* (Macmillan of New York, 1946). One of the most useful volumes on Chinese history. Dependable and rich in information, though dull in style.

E. R. AND K. HUGHES: *Religion in China* (Hutchinson's University Library, 1950). Competent exposition by a lifetime specialist on the subject.

DERK BODDE: *China's Cultural Tradition: What and Whither?* (Rinehart, New York, 1957). Brief and understanding probing into Chinese cultural values.

T. J. HUGHES AND D. E. T. LUARD, *The Economic Development of Communist China, 1949-58* (O.U.P., 1959). One of the best works on this subject, up to the year of the Great Leap Forward.

WANG CHUN-HENG, *A Simple Geography of China* (Collet's, 1959). Concise and illuminating.

A. DOAK BARNETT, *Communist China and Asia* (Council on Foreign Relations, O.U.P., 1960). Scholarly discussion of

the rise of Communist China as a world power, with
particular emphasis on her challenge to American policy.

CHANG-TU HU (ed.), *China: Its People; Its Society; Its Culture*
(HRAF Press, New Haven, 1960). Excellent topical pre-
sentations based on material contributed by scholars at
the University of Washington and Stanford University.
Extensive bibliographical references.

PING-CHIA KUO, *China: New Age and New Outlook* (Penguin,
1960). An objective interpretation of contemporary
China, taking into account the wide range of her
experience and problems.

TIBOR MENDE, *China and Her Shadow* (Thames and Hudson,
1961). Refreshing and unbiassed account by a noted
French political scientist after visiting Communist China.

CURRENT MATERIALS

The People's Handbook published annually in Peking and
China Reconstructs published monthly are handy sources of
general information on Communist China.

FICTION

The following titles may be recommended: Pearl Buck: *The
Good Earth*; John Hersey, *A Single Pebble*; Lu Hsin: *The
True Story of Ah Q*; Lau Shaw: *Ricksha Boy*; Theodore
H. White, *The Mountain Road*.

MAJOR EPOCHS AND EVENTS

I. RISE OF CLASSICAL CHINESE CIVILIZATION

Pre-historical and legendary periods.

c. 1523-c. 1027 B.C.	Shang dynasty.
c. 1027-255 B.C.	Chou dynasty. Confucius.
221-207 B.C.	Ch'in dynasty. The Great Wall.
206 B.C.-220 A.D.	Han dynasty.

II. ENRICHMENT OF CHINESE CIVILIZATION THROUGH CULTURAL FUSION

220-265	Three Kingdoms.
265-317	Chin dynasty.
317-420	Barbarian invasions and East Chin dynasty.
420-589	Northern and Southern dynasties.
589-618	Sui dynasty.
618-906	T'ang dynasty.
907-960	Five ' little dynasties '.

III. MAINTENANCE OF TRADITIONAL SOCIETY DESPITE EXTERNAL CHALLENGES

960-1279	Sung dynasty.
1279-1368	Yüan dynasty. Kublai Khan. Marco Polo.
1368-1644	Ming dynasty.
1644-1820	Earlier phase of Ch'ing dynasty.

IV. COLLAPSE OF OLD ORDER, AND REVOLUTION

A. Later Phase of Ch'ing Dynasty

1839-41	Opium War.		Treaty of Shimonoseki.
1850-65	Taiping Rebellion.	1895	Founding of revolutionary party by Sun Yat-sen.
1858-60	Treaties of Tientsin and Peking.	1898	Scramble for concessions; threatened partition by Powers.
1858-60	Russia in Amur and Ussuri regions.		
1880's	Loss of tributary states in Indo-Chinese peninsula; Russia in Sinkiang.	1898	Hundred Days of Reform.
		1900	Boxer Uprising.
1894-95	Sino-Japanese war;	1911	Revolution, and overthrow of Ch'ing dynasty.

CHINA

B. Revolution, War, and Communism

1912   Founding of Republic.

1913-16   Yüan Shih-kai versus Kuomintang.

1915   Japan's Twenty-one Demands.

1917   Entry into First World War.

1919-26   Civil war among regional warlords.

1919   May 4th Movement.

1921   Founding of Chinese Communist Party.

1924   Reorganization of Kuomintang.

1926   Nationalist Revolution; Rise of Chiang Kai-shek.

1927   Nanking-Wuhan split.

1928   Establishment of Nationalist Government.

1931   'Chinese Soviet Republic', in Kiangsi.

1931   Japanese invasion of Manchuria.

1931-34   Anti-Communist campaigns.

1934-35   The 'Long March'; Yenan.

1935   Japanese attempt to take North China.

1936   Sian coup.

1937   Kuomintang-Communist united front.

1937-45   War against Japan.

1941   Pearl Harbour; War in the Pacific.

1941   Revival of Kuomintang-Communist conflict.

1944-45   Communist demand for coalition.

1945   Japanese surrender.

1946   Marshall mission.

1947-49   Great civil war between Kuomintang and Communists.

1949   Kuomintang defeat on mainland; removal of government to Formosa.

v. NATIONAL RESURGENCE UNDER COMMUNIST REGIME

1949   Establishment of the People's Republic; Chinese People's Political Consultative Conference; 'Common Programme'.

1950   Sino-Soviet Treaty; Korean war.

1950-52   Land Reform movement.

1951   Campaign against Counter-revolutionaries; Communist Army in Tibet; Sino-Tibetan agreement.

1953   Korean armistice.

1953-57   'Socialist Transformation'; First Five Year Plan; Soviet aid on industrial projects.

1954   Constitution; National People's Congress and State Council; Geneva Conference on Indo-China; Formation of SEATO.

1955   Formosa crisis; Bandung Conference; Sino-American ambassadorial talks.

1955-57   Collectivization of agriculture.

1956   Eighth Communist Party Congress; Mediation in Hungarian crisis; Preparatory Committee for Tibetan Autonomous Region.

1958   Great Leap Forward; Commune movement; Crisis over Quemoy and Matsu.

1958-62 'Socialist Construction'; Second Five Year Plan.

1959   Suppression of Tibetan revolt; Boundary dispute with India.

1959-61 Severe droughts and floods; Set-backs in production.

1960-62 Sino-Soviet ideological controversy.

1961   Corrective measures in Communes; Food grain purchases.

1961-62 Laotian crises; Communist guerrillas in Vietnam; border war against India.

INDEX

INDEX

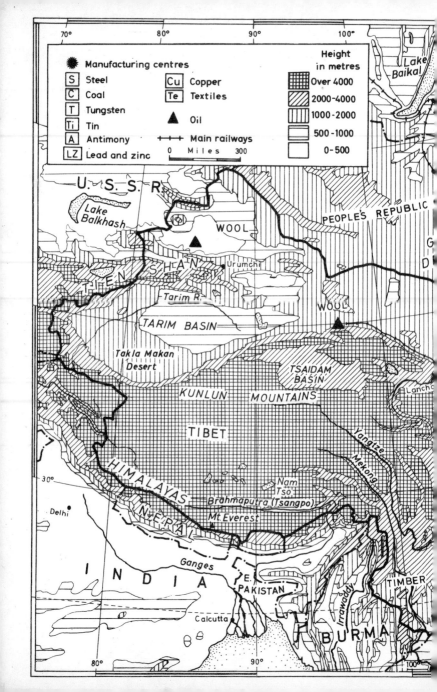